The Future
of Cataloging

Seymour Lubetzky receives his honorary degree from then-Chancellor Charles E. Young at UCLA (1969). At right, Andrew Horn, then-dean of the Graduate School of Library and Information Science.

The Future *of* Cataloging

Insights from the Lubetzky Symposium

April 18, 1998
University of California
Los Angeles

EDITED BY

Tschera Harkness Connell

Robert L. Maxwell

American Library Association
Chicago and London 2000

While extensive effort has gone into ensuring the reliability of information appearing in this book, the publisher makes no warranty, express or implied, on the accuracy or reliability of the information, and does not assume and hereby disclaims any liability to any person for any loss or damage caused by errors or omissions in this publication.

Composition by the dotted i in Sabon and ITC Kabel using QuarkXPress 4.0 on a Macintosh

Printed on 50-pound white offset, a pH-neutral stock, and bound in 10-point coated cover stock by Batson Printing

The paper used in this publication meets the minimum requirements of American National Standard for Information Sciences—Permanence of Paper for Printed Library Materials, ANSI Z39.48-1992. ∞

Library of Congress Cataloging-in-Publication Data
The future of cataloging : insights from the Lubetzky symposium : April 18, 1998, University of California, Los Angeles / edited by Tschera Harkness Connell, Robert L. Maxwell.
      p.   cm.
   Includes index.
   ISBN 0-8389-0778-4
   1. Descriptive cataloging—United States—Congresses.   2. Descriptive cataloging—English-speaking countries—Congresses.   I. Lubetzky, Seymour.   II. Connell, Tschera Harkness.   III. Maxwell, Robert L., 1957–
   Z694.A15 F86   2000
   025.3′2—dc21   99-087247

Printed in the United States of America

04   03   02   01   00   5   4   3   2   1

To Seymour Lubetzky:

When I gained the approval of Mr. MacLeish to appoint a technical assistant I was seeking a person who had demonstrated the qualities of inquisitiveness and mental discipline. I found these reflected in two choice bits on capitalization and title added entries, which had appeared in *The Library Quarterly*. Their author, I decided, was the man for the job. No other decision I have made in five and one-half years has had such important consequences. The report in which I inscribe this note of appreciation to you might never have been written without that decision—certainly not nearly so well. Most of the report is your work; my pride is in having brought you to the Library of Congress. When I leave, I feel greater assurance of continued progress of our work, because I am leaving you behind.

Herman H. Henkle
August 1947

—Inscription by Herman H. Henkle, Director of the Library of Congress Processing Department, in Seymour Lubetzky's copy of *Studies of Descriptive Cataloging: A Report to the Librarian of Congress by the Director of the Processing Department* (Washington, D.C.: Government Printing Office, 1946).

• • • • •

I joined in some intellectual combats with him around the Librarian's Conference table at LC, and developed a high regard for his creative thinking, his tenacious concern to solve a problem, his utter disrespect for impressive authority or tradition, and his complete devotion to the truth and to reason. I hope his arteries never harden.

—Luther H. Evans, Librarian of Congress, in a letter dated September 7, 1955, quoted in Benjamin A. Custer, "Seymour Lubetzky," *Journal of Cataloging & Classification* 12, no. 1 (January 1956): 7.

CONTENTS

The Future of Cataloging

INTRODUCTION

ROBERT L. MAXWELL

On April 18, 1998, a remarkable gathering took place at the Thomas Bradley International Center, University of California, Los Angeles. On that day nearly 250 librarians, students, and other friends and scholars came to southern California, under the auspices of the UCLA Department of Library and Information Science and the UCLA Library and Information Science Alumni Association, to honor one of the most important and beloved thinkers in cataloging theory of the century, Seymour Lubetzky, ten days before his 100th birthday. Attendees had the chance to greet Lubetzky and hear papers read by fourteen cataloging scholars, including one written by Lubetzky himself. This book contains the written version of those presentations.

The presenters spoke of the history and objectives of cataloging and the catalog. They spoke of firmly entrenched principles upon which modern cataloging practice is based. They spoke of the need to tease out the principles upon which the current code, *Anglo-American Cataloguing Rules*, 2nd ed. (AACR2) is implicitly based.[1] Because most of these themes originated with or were amplified by Seymour Lubetzky, it may be appropriate to quote his own summation of them in one of the many revolutionary documents of his career, *Code of Cataloging Rules: Author and Title Entry: An Unfinished Draft*.[2]

> *Objectives*. The objectives which the catalog is to serve are two:
>
> First, to facilitate the location of a particular publication, i.e., of a particular edition of a work, which is in the library.
>
> Second, to relate and display together the editions which a library has of a given work and the works which it has of a given author.
>
> These objectives are complementary in function and both are essential to the effectiveness of the catalog . . . but they also present different requirements which must be reconciled. . . .
>
> *Method*. A work is normally identified and cited by author and title and is, therefore, best entered under author and title in a library catalog. However, the

name of an author and the title of a work are not inherently constant. An author may appear in his various works, and even in the editions of the same work, under different names; and a work may appear in its various editions under different titles. Hence the primary question, (a) whether a given publication, i.e., an edition of a work, should be regarded as a distinct bibliographical entity and represented in the catalog under the name and title by which *it* is identified . . . ; or (b) whether that publication should be regarded as *one of the editions* of a *certain work* by a *certain author,* to be identified by and represented in the catalog under a particular title and a particular name. . . . In the present system the second method is used as far as practicable, because it is consistent with the essential purpose of a publication, which is to present a certain work, and with the essential interest of the users of a publication, which is in the work presented by the publication. It is also a method calculated to produce a catalog which is systematic in structure and efficient in use.

Problems and Principles. The entry of a publication under this system involves the following questions: I. Who is to be regarded as author of the work which a publication presents, particularly if it is prepared by more than one person? II. By which name or form of name is the author to be identified in the catalog if he has used or has had more than one name or more than one form of the name? III. Under which of its parts is the name to be entered in the catalog, particularly if it includes a compound surname or a surname with a prefix? IV. How is that name to be distinguished from similar names of other persons in the catalog? V. By which title should a work be identified in the catalog if issued under more than one title? The answers to these questions will vary under varying circumstances, and they form the substance of the rules, but the various rules are based on the following principles:

I. A work produced by, or issued in the name of, a person or a corporate body is entered under the name of that person or corporate body; a work of multiple authorship is entered under the person or body represented as chiefly responsible for it; a work of complex, changing, doubtful, or unknown authorship is entered under title.

II. An author is normally represented in the catalog under the name and form of the name by which he is most commonly identified in his works, whether that is his real or assumed name, and in the vernacular, except when he has come to be best known in literary and reference sources by another name or designation; an author variously identified in his works is entered preferably under his real name; an author who has changed his name is normally represented under his latest name—except that in the case of a corporate body, which is subject to constitutional changes, a change of name is to be treated as a change of identity.

III. A personal name with a surname is normally entered under the surname; in the case of a compound surname or one with a prefix, the author's own usage or the custom of his country is followed; a corporate name is entered directly in the form used.

IV. The name of a person is distinguished from similar names of others by dates of birth and death, or by the title or designation by which he is commonly identified in his works or in reference sources; the name of a corporate body is distinguished by place of location, community represented or served, date of founding, or other appropriate qualification.

V. The work itself—which is the essence of a publication—whether entered under author or title, is normally represented in the catalog under its original title, except when it has most frequently been issued, or is commonly found in reference sources, under another title; a work whose original title is vague or unknown, or one without an original title, is represented under the title by which it has come to be best known, or under a conventional designation.[3]

Much of this may seem obvious now, but these principles were far from obvious at the time Lubetzky was formulating them. These themes are basic to the cataloging code and to our way of thinking about cataloging at the end of the twentieth century: the twofold objective of the catalog, that of identification and collocation; the work as opposed to the bibliographical item; the principle of authorship; the principle of preferred form of name. Many of the symposium speakers discussed how Lubetzky's principles might hold true in the new, digital world, and a discussion of how well AACR2 has conformed to these principles led to recommendations for change.

Code of Cataloging Rules was prepared as a report to the ALA Catalog Code Revision Committee and it formed the basis of what was to follow, but the reform of the code really got started with Lubetzky's 1953 critique of the 1949 *A.L.A. Cataloging Rules for Author and Title Entries,*[4] when he asked a simple question: "Is this rule necessary?"

Whoever embarks on a study of the development of our cataloging rules, from their spectacular trial before a royal commission and their brilliant defense by Panizzi in 1849 to the appearance of the *A.L.A. Cataloging Rules for Author and Title Entries* in 1949, a round century later, cannot fail to be impressed with the broad knowledge, keen thinking, and fruitful imagination which the founders of the rules have brought to the profession of cataloging. At the same time, one could hardly view with equanimity the continuous proliferation of the rules, their growing complexity, and the obscurement of the objectives and design of the code as a whole. One is impelled to ask: Are all these rules necessary?

> Are all the complexities inevitable? Is there an underlying design which gives our code unity and purpose?
>
> One way to answer these questions and evaluate the structure of our code is to examine the rules one by one and inquire: Is this rule necessary? Is it properly related to the other rules in the code? Is it consistent in purpose and principle with the other rules? Such a task may exact some patience, but it will prove illuminating and rewarding.[5]

Illuminating and rewarding, indeed, and the task taken up and accomplished by Lubetzky has continued to inspire later generations of cataloging theorists, including those whose papers are presented here.

This book is arranged in three parts. The first contains three papers dealing with the history of cataloging theory and Lubetzky's contributions to it. The second consists of reports of current research in cataloging, including research on subject analysis; the performance of current online catalogs with respect to the second objective, collocation; and the work. A thread running through many of these papers is the sudden appearance on the scene of the Internet and the World Wide Web and how cataloging principles might be used to make sense of the mass of information there. In the third section, the authors offer their vision of the future of cataloging and the code.

These are heady times in cataloging. Immediately before the Lubetzky Symposium an international conference was held in Toronto, Ontario, to discuss the future of the code.[6] This conference may prove nearly as important to the history and future of cataloging as the Paris Conference of 1961,[7] and it was discussed in many of the Lubetzky papers, some of whose authors participated in the Toronto Conference. We are reminded of the enduring paradox of the cataloging profession: though it seems to many to be the most prosaic and mechanical aspect of librarianship, it is also the aspect most thoroughly grounded in theory and principles.

As we enter a new century—and millennium—and embark upon what is being called a bright new era, an Information Age, it is appropriate that we stop and reflect on the contributions of this man Seymour Lubetzky to the theory behind the organization of this information, without which we might instead be contemplating a new era of chaos. It is also important that we make sure persons entering the field know of Lubetzky and his contributions, to avoid, in the words of one of the conference participants, "too many catalogers who neither know who Seymour Lubetzky is, nor have an appreciation for the conceptual framework he was so instrumental in creating and upon which their daily labors are based."[8] It is appropriate, then, that we honor Seymour Lubetzky with scholarship showing the directions his guidance beginning more than a half century ago is taking us.

NOTES

1. *Anglo-American Cataloguing Rules,* 2nd ed. (Chicago: American Library Association; London: The Library Association, 1978); 1998 revision (Chicago: American Library Association, 1998).

2. Seymour Lubetzky, *Code of Cataloging Rules: Author and Title Entry: An Unfinished Draft for a New Edition of Cataloging Rules, Prepared for the Catalog Code Revision Committee,* with an explanatory commentary by Paul Dunkin (Chicago: American Library Association, 1960).

3. Lubetzky, *Code of Cataloging Rules,* p. ix–xiii.

4. American Library Association, Division of Cataloging and Classification, *A.L.A. Cataloging Rules for Author and Title Entries,* 2nd ed., ed. Clara Beetle (Chicago: American Library Association, 1949).

5. Seymour Lubetzky, *Cataloging Rules and Principles: A Critique of the A.L.A. Rules for Entry and a Proposed Design for Their Revision* (Washington, D.C.: Library of Congress, 1953; reprint, High Wycombe, England: Published for the College of Librarianship, Wales, by University Microfilms, 1970), p. 1.

6. Proceedings published in Jean Weihs, ed., *The Principles and Future of AACR: Proceedings of the International Conference on the Principles and Future Development of AACR, Toronto, Ontario, Canada, October 23–25, 1997* (Ottawa: Canadian Library Association; London: Library Association Publishing; Chicago: American Library Association, 1998).

7. See International Conference on Cataloguing Principles, *Statement of Principles Adopted at the International Conference on Cataloguing Principles, Paris, October 1961,* annotated ed. with commentary and examples, ed. Eva Verona (London: British Museum; International Federation of Library Associations (Committee on Cataloguing), 1971).

8. See Chapter 9, "The Ideology and Technology of Cataloging at the End of the Millennium," by Maurice J. Freedman.

Select Bibliography
of Publications
by Seymour Lubetzky

"Crisis in the Catalog." *Catalogers' and Classifiers' Yearbook* 8 (1939): 48–54.

"Capital Punishment for Catalogers?" *Library Quarterly* 10, no. 3 (July 1940): 350–60.

"Titles: Fifth Column of the Catalog?" *Library Quarterly* 10, no. 4 (Oct. 1941): 412–30.

Studies of Descriptive Cataloging: A Report to the Librarian of Congress by the Director of the Processing Department (Washington, D.C.: Government Printing Office, 1946).

"The Annex Public Catalog." *LC Information Bulletin* (Dec. 16–22, 1947): 7–8.

"The Official Catalog." *LC Information Bulletin* (Dec. 23–29, 1947): 5–6.

"The Process Information File." *LC Information Bulletin* (Dec. 30, 1947–Jan. 5, 1948): 5–6.

"Cataloging of Publications of Corporate Authors." *Library Quarterly* 21, no. 1 (Jan. 1951): 1–12.

Cataloging Rules and Principles: A Critique of the A.L.A. Rules for Entry and a Proposed Design for Their Revision. Washington, D.C.: Library of Congress, 1953; reprint, High Wycombe, England: Published for the College of Librarianship, Wales, by University Microfilms, 1970.

"Development of Cataloging Rules." *Library Trends* 2, no. 2 (Oct. 1953): 179–86.

"Function of the Catalog." *College and Research Libraries* 17, no. 3 (May 1956): 213–15.

"Non-Author Headings: A Negative Theory." *Journal of Cataloging and Classification* 10, no. 3 (July 1956): 147–54.

"Panizzi vs. the 'Finding Catalog.'" *Journal of Cataloging and Classification* 12, no. 3 (July 1956): 152–56.

Code of Cataloging Rules: Bibliographic Entry and Description: A Partial and Tentative Draft for a New Edition of Bibliographic Cataloging Rules, Prepared for the Catalog Code Revision Committee. [Chicago]: American Library Association, Resources and Technical Services Division, Cataloging and Classification Section, Catalog Code Revision Committee, 1958.

Code of Cataloging Rules: Author and Title Entry: An Unfinished Draft for a New Edition of Cataloging Rules, Prepared for the Catalog Code Revision Committee, with an explanatory commentary by Paul Dunkin. Chicago: American Library Association, 1960.

"The Current Revision of ALA Rules." *Library Resources & Technical Services* 4, no. 1 (Winter 1960): 79–84.

"Smoke over Revision." *Library Journal* 86, no. 15 (Sept. 1, 1961): 2740–44.

Re Dewton's Paper: "The Paris Cataloging Principles." Washington, D.C.: Library of Congress, 1961.

"Cataloging Made Easy?" *Library Journal* 87, no. 18 (Oct. 15, 1962): 3647–48.

"Compromise in Cataloging." *Library Journal* 88, no. 1 (Jan. 1, 1963): 46.

"Quest for Catalogers: Today and Tomorrow." *Library Journal* 88, no. 17 (Oct. 1, 1963): 3535–38.

"The Library Catalog: Focus on Form." *Library Resources & Technical Services* 8, no. 3 (Summer 1964): 317–22.

"Lubetzky vs. Dewey." *Library Journal* 89, no. 15 (Sept. 1, 1964): 3054–56.

"Catalog Code Revision, 1964." *Library Journal* 89, no. 22 (Dec. 15, 1964): 4863–65, 4870.

"On Teaching Cataloging." *Journal of Education for Librarianship* 5, no. 4 (Spring 1965): 255–58.

"Sears without Dewey." *Library Journal* 91, no. 3 (Feb. 1, 1966): 672–74.

Bibliographic Dimensions of Information Control, with R. M. Hayes. Report 1 of a series on the Principles of Cataloging. Los Angeles: University of California Institute of Library Research, 1968.

The Author and Title Catalog in the Library: Its Role, Function, and Objectives. Report 2 of a series on the Principles of Cataloging. Los Angeles: University of California Institute of Library Research, 1969.

Descriptive Cataloging: Problems and Principles. Report 3 of a series on the Principles of Cataloging. Los Angeles: Institute of Library Research, University of California, April 1969.

Principles of Cataloging: Final Report, Phase I: Descriptive Cataloging. Los Angeles: University of California Institute of Library Research, 1969.

To Seymour Lubetzky on the Occasion of His First Centennial

ELAINE SVENONIUS

On this occasion of celebration
Let there be time for deliberation.
The question before us—we must make sure—
What in cataloging is meant to endure?
The answer surely is easy to find:
Quite simply it's Seymour Lubetzky's mind.

Principled, purposed in its endeavor
What it created will live forever:
Each book to a work must connect.
This each reader has a right to expect.
If objectives are not to be abrogated
The edifice must be integrated.

The truths Panizzi adumbrated
Seymour Lubetzky elevated.
Holding a prism to his teacher's light
He refracted it with words aimed right
Creating a pristine ideology
Unsullied by changing technology.

The ideas for which his followers grope
No more than turns of his kaleidoscope;
Nor entries added to the diary of mankind
But references to the work of his fine mind.
In the catalog of those who are truly great
He's the main entry—let's celebrate!

The History of Cataloging and the Contributions of Seymour Lubetzky

1

The Vicissitudes of Ideology and Technology in Anglo-American Cataloging since Panizzi and a Prospective Reformation of the Catalog for the Next Century

SEYMOUR LUBETZKY

in collaboration with

ELAINE SVENONIUS

This report was intended to begin with a perspective on what occurred in Anglo-American cataloging since Antonio Panizzi—the man who started it all when he appeared in London at the British Museum and brought a new vision and meaning to the concepts of the book, the library, and the catalog forming the complex of librarianship. But to understand what occurred, it is necessary to take cognizance of the two pivotal events that have influenced and shaped the course and character of Anglo-American cataloging. One of these, the first and most important, involved Panizzi. This was the appointment in 1847 of a commission named Commissioners Appointed to Inquire into the Constitution and Government of the British Museum, briefly referred to as the Royal Commission. The hearings held by the Commission from 1847 to 1849 ranged broadly over the administration and affairs of the British Museum. But the cause of, and the reason for, the appointment of the Commission and the most important, interesting, dramatic, and consequential part of the hearings was a heated debate of Panizzi's cataloging rules.

Delivered on the occasion of Seymour Lubetzky's centennial celebration at the Bradley Center, UCLA, April 18, 1998

The issue exploded in 1841.

Toward the end of the 1830s, the interleaved catalog of the British Museum library was overcrowded with entries, out of alphabetical order, and without room for incoming new entries. There was a crying need for a new edition of the catalog and Panizzi, Keeper of the Department of Printed Books—that is, the library—was urgently ordered by the Trustees to prepare a new edition of the catalog. To do so expeditiously, Panizzi was expected to cut up the catalog, arrange the entries in correct alphabetical order, mount them on boards, and give them to the printer as copy for the new edition.

When the eagerly awaited first volume of what was expected to be the new edition of the catalog appeared in 1841, it stunned, confounded, and angered the library establishment and the library community generally. It also offended many that a "foreigner," who was granted asylum and a respectable job in the British Museum, should so insensitively disregard the rules, traditions, and customs of the British librarians and library users, and inflict upon them a totally strange kind of catalog unlike any they had ever seen or heard of.

How did Panizzi's rules differ from those previously used in the British Museum and elsewhere?

Interestingly, they differed primarily, and basically, in view of what the book represents. The traditional rules saw the books of the library as discrete entities, and the catalog as a record designed to help one find the book desired under its author's name, title of the book, or any other clue under which a reader might reasonably look for it. Panizzi's rules conceived of *books* as editions of particular *works*, with those representing the same work to be integrated and arranged in the catalog in a prescribed order, so that the reader who came to the library for a particular book would find it in context with other books representing editions of the same work and might select the edition or editions that would best serve his or her interests.

To achieve that purpose, Panizzi ruled that "No work ever to be entered twice at full length. Whenever requisite, cross-references to be introduced" (Rule LIV).[1] Thus, editions of a work issued under different names of the author or different titles should not be entered separately under the names or titles as issued, but should be entered in the catalog under one name of the author and one title, with references used to inform the reader where the book or edition sought was to be found. And here is the origin of what eventually were recognized and adopted at the

International Conference on Cataloguing Principles in Paris, in 1961, as the two fundamental objectives of the catalog: (1) to help a reader find a particular book which the library may have; and (2) to reveal to the reader at the same time what editions and translations the library may have of the work, and what works it may have of the author.[2] These objectives relate to the dichotomous character of the book, which, extrinsically, is a separate physical entity, an artifact unrelated to any other, but, intrinsically, a record of human thought and experience, related to other records of the author with which it should be integrated. The objectives of identification and integration of the books of a library are fundamental to the design of an effective catalog and are unlikely to be affected by any future development. They should also be the fundamental objectives of the catalog of the next century.

But when Panizzi's rules appeared in 1841, they showed a plain disregard of those of his predecessor, which had been handed him when he was ordered to prepare the new edition of the British Museum catalog and was told to follow them. Panizzi was roundly denounced and excoriated. He decided to ask for two things: (1) that the publication of his maligned catalog be discontinued; and (2) that an impartial commission be appointed before whom he could meet his detractors and answer their criticism and complaints. Both requests were granted, and in 1847 the Royal Commission was appointed and witnesses came forward to air their opinions and feelings about the British Museum and the Keeper of the Department of Printed Books.

The witnesses represented the elite and most prominent in the community. A few came to speak in support of Panizzi, but the rest were almost unanimously opposed to him. Among the latter was Panizzi's arch foe but most prestigious witness, Thomas Carlyle. Carlyle had a longstanding feud with Panizzi, complaining that he was not given the attention and help he needed in his work by Panizzi's staff in the British Museum library. Panizzi replied that Carlyle got the same attention and help that every other user of the library received—which was hardly calculated to appease Carlyle. At the hearings of the Royal Commission, Carlyle appeared as an eminent scholar and longtime user of the catalogs of the British Museum library, who, by virtue of his own experience, was deemed especially well qualified to pass judgment about catalogs generally and Panizzi's cataloging rules in particular. So when the presiding commissioner, the Earl of Ellesmere, turned to Carlyle and asked him what he thought about the functions of a library catalog and what that requires, Carlyle rose and authoritatively declared: "A library is not worth anything without a catalogue—it is a Polyphemus without any eye in his head—and you must front the difficulties, whatever they may be, of making proper catalogues"(Q 4472). But he went on to emphasize that "The grand use of any catalogue is to tell you, in any intelligible way, that such and such books are in the library. . . . I should expect it to be a simple thing enough to draw up a list of the names of the books" (Q 4385).[3] Carlyle argued that the book is normally provided with a title page, which serves to name and identify it, and by which it is commonly cited, referred to, and looked for by a reader at the catalog. It should therefore accordingly be entered in the catalog to tell the reader right at the outset whether or not the library has the book wanted, rather than send the reader to look for the information elsewhere in the catalog.

Panizzi's response was, in effect: Yes, I require the reader to look in two places for the information he wants, because I want to tell him much more than merely whether or not the library has a particular book; yes, my rules are complicated, but that is because my rules are concerned not only with the book as a single and separate item, but also as part of a complex of editions and translations of potential interest to an inquiring reader; and yes, my rules will make cataloging more costly, but that cost is only a onetime cost to enhance the quality of the catalog and benefit the library and its users for an indefinite time in the future. In Panizzi's own words, "a reader may know the *work* he requires; but he cannot be expected to know all the peculiarities of different *editions*, and this information he has a right to expect from the catalogues"(Q 9814). So here we have two individuals looking at the same object—the book—but seeing different things. Carlyle saw the book as a material object, a separate entity unrelated to any other book in the library, and he did not see why it should not be so represented in the catalog. Panizzi saw the book as an edition of a particular work that is intimately related to the other editions and translations of the work that the library may have, and thought that it should therefore be *integrated* with them. How come? Simply because the book is a dichotomous object. Extrinsically, it is an artifact; but intrinsically, it is a record of human experience. And Panizzi urged recognition of the fact that the essence of a book is not its form but its contents, and that this consideration should determine the character of the catalog.

Panizzi, however, as a librarian himself, burdened by many other mundane problems, realized that Carlyle's call for a simple catalog that could be produced easily, quickly, and inexpensively, and would more readily be understood by and responsive to the plain requests of its users, was the siren song that would allure most librarians. They would argue that a catalog that was good and sufficient for a scholar of the stature of Carlyle should be good and sufficient enough for all readers. He felt, though, that the Commissioners, detached from the librarians' daily problems, would dispassionately consider the merits of his effort. So he sat down and wrote a very lengthy and detailed letter to the Earl of Ellesmere seeking to convey an insight into the intricacies of the problems of cataloging and their implications.[4] When the Commissioners concluded their investigations and hearings, they issued a report explaining their findings and recommendations—including one for the Trustees not to meddle in or interfere with Panizzi's work in matters of cataloging—reserving for the end an implicitly significant note:

> We must fairly confess that our inquiries, especially into the whole subject of the catalogue, lead us to doubt whether there is not some hazard in the practice of interfering in the details of the library on the part of the board . . . We have had occasion, in the course of our inquiry, to ascertain the prevalence among many persons of an impression which attributes to that gentleman [Mr. Panizzi] not only the adoption of a plan for a catalogue, of which these parties . . . disapprove, but also the delay of which they complain in the execution of the plan as adopted. It becomes our incidental duty to do him justice in these particulars. From what we have already stated it will appear that, with respect to the system and form of the catalogue, whatever be its defects, Mr. Panizzi can be charged with nothing further than the constant approval and acceptance of one leading principle, that of fulness and accuracy . . . If completed, with any near approach to the perfection which its plan and rules contemplate, it will form a record to future times of great value of the printed literature of the period which it embraces[5]

—a triumphant vindication of Panizzi, who stood by his principles, unbowed by unmitigated criticism and unending carping by hostile opponents.

This, then, concludes the history of the first pivotal event in modern Anglo-American cataloging. It concerned itself primarily with the ideological foundation of the catalog—the fundamental problem of what were to be the objectives that the catalog of a library should be designed to serve and the methods of achieving them. And it influenced the discussions and the course of Anglo-American cataloging since (witness the perennial discussions of the functions of the main entry devised by Panizzi).

The second pivotal event in the history of Anglo-American cataloging was the introduction of technology in cataloging to enhance its effectiveness. This occurred at the turn of the century, when the Library of Congress, in a visionary mood, announced that it was making its printed catalog cards available to all libraries at a cost to cover merely that of the paper and the distribution of the cards. In contrast to the hostility that greeted Panizzi's rules, the offer was instantly recognized as one of incalculable potentialities and a boon to all libraries. To begin with, it would immediately relieve the libraries of almost their total task and cost of cataloging. It would automatically be productive, for the first time in the history of Anglo-American cataloging, of a national cataloging standard. It would make possible and facilitate establishing local, regional, and other kinds of union catalogs—all as a result of using a national cataloging standard. And beyond that was the prospect for bibliographical communication and cooperation, not only nationally but also internationally— particularly among English-speaking countries.

The Library of Congress introduced the first use of technology in cataloging, and its success generated a penchant for the use of technology that has continued to date, without, however, an obvious awareness that technology is not an end in itself, but a means to an end. When, in an enthusiasm for technology, the end—that is, the objective of a pursuit—is lost sight of, the technology is miscarried.

The Library of Congress's offer to make its catalog cards available to all libraries was timely, farsighted, and statesmanlike. Prior to that offer every library did its own cataloging and was not able to cooperate and share results of its work. The Library of Congress's offer immediately made interlibrary cooperation possible, and in 1961, a little more than half a century later, led to the first fully international cataloging agreements—an advance in cataloging from a cottage industry to an international one.

A conspicuous advance in the use of technological capacity to resolve cataloging problems was the introduction of the online catalog. Traditionally, a book is identified first by the name of the author given on the title page, and is accordingly entered in the catalog. That seems simple and reasonable, but there is a hidden and unyielding snag to confound the user of the catalog. This happens because the names of individuals are customarily construed and used differently in different countries, with the result that similar and identical names are entered differently in the catalog. This is particularly true in the case of compound names and names with prefixes such as *von* and *de*. Thus, for example, Wernher von Braun, as a U.S. citizen, is entered in the catalog as Von Braun, Wernher, but if the same Wernher von Braun were a German citizen, his name would have to be entered in the catalog as Braun, Wernher von. Now how would a reader be helped to find the book he or she wants under such circumstances? This is where the online catalog comes in. Using the capacity of the computer to retrieve a certain book by means of a few uncommon elements from the title page obviates the whole problem incidental to the use of the author's name. But note that the online catalog serves only the first objective of the catalog—to help the reader find the particular book he or she wants. If the capacity of the online catalog could be enhanced to reveal also the second objective—to reveal to the reader also what editions and translations the library has of a particular work and what works the library has of a particular author—that would be a crowning achievement of the pursuit of technological capacity in cataloging, an indispensable link in the chain of transmission of the records of civilization.

But, now, what about the details in the shape of our rules? The major aspects of a pursuit normally engage the best minds, but the details tend to be neglected, ignored, or left for others to concern themselves with. And yet we know how important a detail can be, that for the want of a nail a war was lost, and that a misconceived improvement of a rule may vitiate the whole objective of that rule. So, with this in mind, we want to look at some of the details of our code for guidance in preparing the next catalog.

As mentioned earlier, Panizzi's stark rule prescribing only one entry, with references, for a book, and barring the use of added entries, was deemed unduly rigorous, particularly by those who previously were using the title-added entry as an effective aid in locating a book. So when the 1908 rules were being prepared, it was decided to provide for the use of both, the main entry and added entries.[6] This decision has been followed since, without any questioning. But was it a sound and helpful decision, one to be continued and followed in the catalog of the next century? Or was it the result of a misunderstanding and misjudgment of Panizzi's ideology and his plan of the catalog?

Remember that, for Panizzi, a book is not a separate entity, but an edition or translation of a particular work and, accordingly, is to be integrated and represented in the catalog together with all the other editions and translations of the work that the library might have. That is the purpose of Panizzi's main entry. The use of an added entry—e.g., a title-added entry—would vitiate the purpose of the main entry. For if a reader looked in the catalog under the title of the book he or she wants and finds it there, that would end the search without his or her learning about other editions that the library might have. Again, if the reader did not find the book he or she wants under its title, he or she would have to assume that the book is not in the library, without learning that the library might have other editions of the work that could equally well, or even better, serve his or her purposes. That is how the use of an added entry is inevitably misleading for the user of the catalog, why Panizzi barred strictly the use of added entries, and why the decision in the 1902 rules to use both main entries and added entries was ill-advised and has impaired the integrity of Anglo-American cataloging since. It should now be discontinued as a case of misjudgment.[7]

Another detail affecting an intelligent use of our rules is their catechismal character. They tell the cataloger what, when, and how to do in certain circumstances, but not why. If a cataloger is to perform his or her work thoughtfully and interestedly, he or she should have a comprehensive idea of what the work is all about. This could readily be achieved by providing a concise introduction to the rules, explaining the importance and role of the catalog, the objectives to be served, the problems involved, and the rules developed to implement the objectives. The draft *Code of Cataloging Rules* provides an example.[8] It is particularly important that the rules for the catalog of the next century be prefaced with such an introduction.[9]

Certainly, these details do not exhaust all the potential for improvement in the quality of our rules, but they indicate how much room is left for improvement in the rules for the next century. Cataloging is an indispensable link in the transmission, integration, and exploration of the records of human civilization. It is central to all operations and services and to the whole mission of the library. And it should be kept in optimal condition—ideologically, methodologically, and technologically—to serve well the library of the twenty-first century.

NOTES

1. Anthony Panizzi, "Rules for the Compilation of the Catalogue," in British Museum, Dept. of Printed Books, *Catalogue of Printed Books in the British Museum* (London: Printed by Order of the Trustees, 1841), vol. 1, p. v–ix, reprinted in *Foundations of Cataloging: A Sourcebook,* ed. Michael Carpenter and Elaine Svenonius (Littleton, Colo.: Libraries Unlimited, 1985), p. 1–14.

2. International Federation of Library Associations, *Report. Proceedings of the International Conference on Cataloguing Principles, Paris, 9th–18th October, 1961* (London: International Federation of Library Associations, 1962), 91–92. The objectives are paraphrased in this paper.

3. Commissioners Appointed to Inquire into the Constitution and Government of the British Museum, *Report of the Commissioners Appointed to Inquire into the Constitution and Government of the British Museum, with Minutes of Evidence* (London: Her Majesty's Stationery Office, 1850). Question numbers in the text reference the *Minutes of Evidence.*

4. Anthony Panizzi, "Mr. Panizzi to the Right Hon. The Earl of Ellesmere. British Museum, 29 January 1848," in Commissioners Appointed to Inquire into the Constitution and Government of the British Museum, *Appendix to the Report of the Commissioners Appointed to Inquire into the Constitution and Management of the British Museum* (London: Her Majesty's Stationery Office, 1850), 378–95, reprinted in *Foundations of Cataloging,* p. 18–47.

5. Commissioners Appointed to Inquire into the Constitution and Government of the British Museum, *Report,* p. 16, 19.

6. *Cataloguing Rules: Author and Title Entries,* English ed. (London: The Library Association, 1908); *Catalog Rules: Author and Title Entries,* American ed. (Chicago: American Library Association, 1908).

7. For a discussion of this detail, see Chapter 6, "Main and Added Entries," by Michael Carpenter.

8. Seymour Lubetzky, *Code of Cataloging Rules: Author and Title Entry: An Unfinished Draft for a New Edition of Cataloging Rules, Prepared for the Catalog Code Revision Committee,* with an explanatory commentary by Paul Dunkin (Chicago: American Library Association, 1960).

9. For discussions of this detail, see Chapter 12, "Cataloging at Crossroads: Preservation and Accommodation," by John D. Byrum, Jr., and Chapter 13, "Guidelines for a Future Anglo-American Cataloging Code," by Margaret F. Maxwell.

2

Seymour Lubetzky, Man of Principles

MICHAEL GORMAN

I praise Seymour Lubetzky and will, of necessity, discuss some hardcore cataloguing matters that I hope will not offend the bibliographically faint of heart.

The English literary critic F. R. Leavis wrote extensively on the Great Tradition of the English novel, which, if memory serves, began with George Eliot and ended with D. H. Lawrence. English-language descriptive cataloguing has its own Great Tradition—a tradition that began with Antonio Panizzi's "91 rules"[1] and reached its most recent peak in the work of Seymour Lubetzky. Because of his influence and the power of his ideas, it can truly be said that the most suitable title for a history of Anglo-American cataloguing would be "From Panizzi to Lubetzky."

I was in Rome in March of 1998. On the morning of the day I left, I took a walk in the gardens of the Villa Borghese. One tree-lined avenue was also lined with plinths on which rested busts of eminent Italians, all but one, alas, unknown to me. The one that I did recognize sported the aquiline, noble features of Antonio Panizzi, the preeminent giant of the First Age of English-language cataloguing. It is one of the ironies of history that both Seymour Lubetzky (who was born in Zelwa in what is now Belarus) and his nineteenth-century counterpart were born far from the Anglo-American world. Panizzi was a revolutionary in fractured nineteenth-century Italy who fled his country to escape the Austrian princeling who ruled the Duchy of Modena. He arrived in liberal England penniless and barely able to speak English, but through using his intellect and his determination completed the transition from Antonio to Sir Anthony by becoming one of the most eminent Victorians—the creator of Great Britain's de facto national library and, in many ways, the inventor of the modern national library idea. He also created the Iron Library and the famous round Reading Room of the British Museum and went on to write his "91 rules" in ten days! (Something to think of in times when it takes years to approve a single rule change in AACR2.)

Though Panizzi is, indisputably, the giant of nineteenth-century English-language descriptive cataloguing, he is the first among equals in that period of what I call the First Age of descriptive cataloguing—the age of the single-author code. Is it a coincidence that those single-author codes (including those of Cutter[2] and Jewett[3]) shared some positive characteristics? They were all brief, written in simple declarative English, and, most important, based on a principled approach. We who are now in the Third Age of descriptive cataloguing would do well to ponder the nature and value of those single-author codes and to seek to apply their values to our own work. With an almost uncanny chronological exactitude, the First Age ended with the life of Queen Victoria on the appointment of the U.S. and British committees for what became the 1908 code.[4] The Second Age that followed was the era of the committee code, the increasingly loose, baggy monsters that began with the *Cataloguing Rules* of 1908 and ended with the publication of the two texts of the *Anglo-American Catalog[u]ing Rules* in 1967.[5] Although the latter is nominally the first of a new era of codes, even cursory study will show that its name promises more than it delivers, and that the name *Anglo-American Cataloguing Rules,* 2nd ed. (AACR2) for the 1978 code is a major misnomer that has had malign results.[6]

Before dealing with the first AACR and the events that led up to its failure, here is a brief history of the Second Age. The 1908 rules were the product of two committees (British and American) and though the codes published in the two countries were substantially similar, the texts contained both alternative rules (for matters on which the American and British committees could not agree) and statements of alternative Library of Congress (LC) practice and LC "supplementary rules." Without even going into the deficiencies of the rules themselves, we can see here a major problem of the "committee code"—the inability to reconcile differing opinions, particularly in the absence of mastering principles or even an agreed basis for decision. One notable, and negative, aspect of the 1908 code is its infamous distinction between societies (entered under their names) and institutions (entered under their places), which was bad enough in itself but also gave rise to an alternative rule for societies "whose names include that of some locality" (to be entered under place). Then there is the burgeoning of the "case-law" rules. To take just a few examples, we find rules for chrestomathies, heraldic visitations, thematic catalogues, architectural plans, papal bulls, epitomes, and exploring expeditions (the latter is a two-part rule, the second of which has no fewer than six subrules). The point about this baroque extravagance is not only that the rules are unnecessary but also that they are internally contradictory in the absence of guiding principles. An architect's plans are to be entered under the name of the architect (the obvious author), but an epitome is to be entered under the author of the work epitomized (equally obviously not the author). One could go on but my point is not to mock the work of the worthies who so toiled but to emphasize the importance of guiding principles and the serious problems caused by their absence.

As the Second Age of descriptive cataloguing rolled on, things got worse. The Vatican code of 1931 was compiled almost entirely by American librarians and contained, as it claimed, "the most complete statement of American cataloging practice."[7] Alas, it was only available in Italian until the second edition was translated into English and circulated in 1939, though not published until 1948.[8] Those are dates with some resonance in Europe and, in any event, British and American committees were already at work by that time on a revision of the 1908 rules. The British committee members were otherwise occupied after September of 1939, and the American group went on alone to produce the Draft code of 1941[9]—a code that is remembered now only because it gave rise to the scathing criticism of the Australian Andrew Osborne in his justly famous article "Crisis in Cataloging" that same year.[10] Osborne's targets were greater than the Draft code itself, but his article included some themes that were to be amplified later by Lubetzky. To summarize, Osborne called for rules that were relatively few in number and simpler because they would not cover rare cases and would be pruned of inessential matter; and for training for cataloguers that would allow them to use their judgment based on understood principles embodied in the rules. Osborne's paper is rare for it was well received both by those with a theoretical interest in cataloguing and by library administrators—a fragile coalition that fell apart before the 1967 AACR was published. What a pity his wise words were not heeded. Had they been, cataloguing might have progressed to the point at which the disastrous 1949 rules and the half-hearted revision of 1967 might have been avoided.

Be that as it may, the fact is that Osborne's illuminating paper was ignored by the cataloguing establishment of the time and the American committee forged ahead with the preparation of the 1949 publication, *A.L.A. Cataloging Rules for Author and Title Entries.*[11] Unlike the 1908 code, the 1949 code did not include rules for bibliographic description, which was left to the *Rules for Descriptive Cataloging in the Library of Congress,* published in the same year.[12] The 1949 rules (the "Red book") were never adopted in Britain, and the British were left to soldier on with the 1908 rules, trying to apply Edwardian cases to publications of the 1950s and 1960s. As a young cataloguer in the early 1960s, the inadequacies of the case-law approach were made manifest to me every day and the thirst for a Lubetzkian code grew ever stronger. In some ways the 1949 rules were better than the 1908 rules (better organized, more up-to-date examples, etc.), but in other ways they were worse. This is not to fault those who framed the rules because the rules were the logical result of a faulty premise. For example, the complications of the distinction between "societies" and "institutions" were magnified as (in the words of John Horner), the categories were "sub-categorised, exemplified, and excepted to the point of confusion—because, of course, the wrong characteristics are used to establish the categories . . . and then attempts made to sub-categorise; until one finishes up with individually named buildings having rules of their own."[13] (The latter seems almost inconceivable but, sure enough, rule 116B(3) is devoted to and only to the Basilian Monastery at Mount Sinai!) Another major fault of the 1949 rules is the degree to which the rules are subjective. The cataloguer, for instance, is instructed to enter works published under a pseudonym under the real name *except* when the pseudonym "has become fixed in literary history" or when current authors are "better known by pseudonym than by real name." These subjective judgments are not assisted by the example of a work by Mark Twain entered under "[Clemens, Samuel Langhorne . . .]," but a work by George Sand entered under that name. Is the latter example really more "fixed in literary history" than the former? Who is to judge and by which criteria?

The 1949 rules, here and elsewhere, were thus set up following Os-borne's advice to allow the cataloguer more discretion. Discretion with-out guiding principles, however, can never produce standard results. The situation following the adoption of the 1949 rules combined the worst of several worlds. Cataloguers were given options and asked to make sub-jective decisions without guidance; there was no longer an Anglo-Ameri-can agreement on descriptive cataloguing; and the worst aspects of the case-law approach still ruled. Cometh the hour, cometh the man!

The hour was the low point of the Second Age of cataloguing and the man, of course, was Seymour Lubetzky. The first general publication of his ideas was in the 1946 Library of Congress *Studies of Descriptive Cataloging*,[14] but it was in 1953 that he really made his mark. It is in-disputable that the most influential publication of the century in this field was his 1953 pamphlet *Cataloging Rules and Principles*.[15] Written for the ALA Division of Cataloging and Classification at the behest of the Library of Congress (though not received at LC with universal ap-probation), the pamphlet had an enormous influence on the develop-ment of descriptive cataloguing in the Anglo-American world and beyond. It can still be read with profit today and is, far and away, the major influence on AACR2. In *Cataloging Rules and Principles*, Sey-mour Lubetzky wielded Occam's Razor to devastating effect. His para-phrase of the fourteenth-century philosopher's wisdom was "Is this rule necessary?"—a seemingly simple question that blew the 1949 rules out of the water. In instance upon instance, Seymour Lubetzky showed that rules were unnecessary, were not related to the other rules, and were in-consistent in purpose and principle with the other rules in the code. When dealing with the tangle of rules dealing with "societies" and "in-stitutions," for example, Lubetzky looked at the historical reasons why cataloguers had been saddled with this mess and concluded that the dis-tinction had never made sense and could never make sense. It is a fun-damental of Eastern thought for the sage to ask questions that are simultaneously wise and childlike. In 1953, cataloguing's sage created a revolution by asking questions such as "Why?" and "What is this for?"

In the section of his pamphlet that dealt with the design of a new code (and a new kind of code), Seymour Lubetzky defines two objec-tives of the catalogue in the following words: "The first objective is to enable the user of the catalog to determine readily whether or not the li-brary has the book he wants. . . . The second objective is to reveal to the user of the catalog, under one form of the author's name, what works the library has by a given author and what editions or translations of a given work."[16] These are, of course, restatements of Charles A. Cutter's "Objects," but they are not limited by Cutter's concern for the "convenience of the public." As Paul Dunkin pointed out, however, they are statements of what the writer believes best serves that convenience.[17] The objectives are also significant for they clearly distinguish between "books" (i.e., publications, bibliographic items that form the basis of description) and "works" (abstractions of which "books" are manifestations and that are the basis of assigning headings/access points that are used to fulfill both objectives). This distinction is the basis for AACR2, though, I would readily admit, not always carried out impeccably in that publication.

Cataloging Rules and Principles was well received by cataloguers and was the primary impetus for establishing yet another Cataloging Code Revision Committee in 1954 (significantly a few scant years after the 1949 code—a haste that can only be explained by the two-pronged criticism from Seymour Lubetzky and fed-up cataloguers). In 1956, Lubetzky was named editor of the proposed revision. In 1951, the British Library Association had appointed a committee to work on a revision of the 1908 rules (as I have said, the 1949 code was never adopted in the UK) and the committees agreed to work together (and with the Canadian Library Association committee) toward a new, Lubetzkian joint cataloguing code. These were heady times. It seemed that an unprecedented era of international agreement on a principle-based code that would provide better catalogues and better cataloguing for the English-speaking world was upon us. This feeling was reinforced by the 1960 draft *Code of Cataloging Rules*[18] and the 1961 International Conference on Cataloguing Principles, which resulted in a statement known informally as the Paris Principles.[19] The 1960 draft was, of course, written by Seymour Lubetzky and the 1961 principles leaned heavily on his work. It must have seemed that the revolution was complete but, alas, Osborne's alliance between administrators and cataloguers was beginning to come apart.

The original idea was to produce a good, principle-based code and to worry about the cost of change (real and imaginary) later. It became evident in national institutes held by the revision committee and, indeed, in some aspects of the 1960 draft itself that cost considerations were beginning to have an impact. Led by the LC and the Association of Research Libraries (ARL), American research library administrators brought pressure to bear on the Committee to reject certain provisions that would, in their view, cost too much to implement. Seymour Lubetzky resigned as editor in 1962 and work proceeded on the spavined compromise that became the *Anglo-American Catalog[u]ing Rules* of 1967. (Note the brackets around the "u" in the word "catalog[u]ing." They are symbolic of the fact that the British committee rejected the LC/ARL-enforced compromises and published a separate "British text" of AACR that, though still flawed, followed most of the Lubetzkian principles.) The revolution had failed, temporarily at least, and that was a sorry thing for at least two reasons. The first is that cataloguing was still lumbered with compromise and case laws and catalogues grew even more convoluted and difficult to use. Those who care about the cost of cataloguing change rarely reflect on the cost of *not* changing—a cost in time and money that is borne by every catalogue user and that increases with every day an inadequate cataloguing code is used. The second reason for sorrow over the 1967 code is that it coincided almost exactly with the birth of machine-readable cataloguing (MARC), which, though few realised it at the time, would be the cause of the demise of the card catalogue for which the AACR compromise was made. Just think of the quality of our databases today if MARC records, from the outset, had been based on a coherent, principled, Lubetzkian code!

I have neither the time nor the inclination to go into the many shortcomings of the 1967 code, and will content myself with observing that, although the Lubetzkian revolution had been stymied for a time, external forces—notably the MARC-driven need for a single Anglo-American cataloguing code and the promulgation and rapid international adoption of the International Standard Bibliographic Descriptions (ISBDs)—were making another revision inevitable and that sooner rather than later.

Political compromises were made over AACR2 as well, notably over the pretence that this was a "second edition" of the 1967 code, when it was nothing of the sort. The same reactionary forces that brought down the 1967 code tried again and may well have been successful if AACR2 had a name that indicated how much of a break with the past it really was. On the other hand, if the 1978 code had a new name, we could have been spared all those tedious "AACR3" discussions. Despite the compromises and flaws in execution, I will always believe that AACR2 represents the triumph of the logic and analysis of Seymour Lubetzky. I am proud to have been associated with it and to have played a part in bringing the major part of the Lubetzkian revolution to fruition.

I would like to close by mentioning the most enduring of the cataloguing principles with which Lubetzky is associated—the principle of authorship. This has been a bedrock of all the English-language cataloguing codes in the Great Tradition and is, I firmly believe, one that has permanent validity. Its application has become muddied by me, among others, because the *principle* of authorship has been confused with a concept of catalogue organization—the "main entry." I have thought about these matters for many years, not least because they have been the cause of what appears to be a difference of views between Seymour Lubetzky and me. I would like to use this opportunity to try to explain the view I now hold and, thus, remove even an appearance of difference. Put as simply as I can, I believe the principle of authorship—the idea that one's first consideration on assigning access points/headings to a work should be to discover the author(s) of that work—is as valid today as it has ever been. Without it, the catalogue becomes a random assemblage of access points that may be standard in *form* but do not carry out Seymour Lubetzky's objectives of the catalogue. To me this is a very different matter from the manner in which the catalogue is organized. In using the principle of authorship to determine one or more access points, one need not be choosing one of those access points over the other as far as *the organization and the use* of the catalogue are concerned. In other words, the determination of the author of a work does not lead inevitably to that author's access point being different from other access points *in the catalogue.* In cases in which a work is given a uniform title, that title will, of course, be associated with the access point for the author, but, again, such an association does not mean that name/title combination is treated differently from other access points in the catalogue. There are subsidiary uses for the idea of the main entry (single-author listings and Cutter numbers come to mind), but these are not part of the organization and the use of the catalogue. In short, doing away with the idea of the "main entry" as an organizational principle of the catalogue does *not* involve abandoning the principle of authorship. I hope that future revisions of AACR2 will contain wording that makes this point clear.

I have not spoken of Seymour Lubetzky's teaching at UCLA after 1962, but I know that he was a great and loved teacher in a time when library schools (to use the, unfortunately, old-fashioned term) regarded cataloguing as a central part of library education. Here again we see the happy coincidence of the time and the man to the direct benefit of his students and faculty colleagues and the indirect benefit of the profession of librarianship.

When AACR2 was first published, I was honoured to be asked to inscribe Seymour Lubetzky's copy. I copied T. S. Eliot's dedication of

The Wasteland to Ezra Pound and inscribed it to *il miglior fabbro* (the better artificer). As a maker of cataloguing rules and as a cataloguing theoretician, Seymour Lubetzky is unrivaled and all of us who are involved in cataloguing are forever in his debt.

NOTES

1. "Rules for the Compilation of the Catalogue," in British Museum, Dept. of Printed Books, *Catalogue of Printed Books in the British Museum* (London: Printed by Order of the Trustees, 1841), vol.1, p. v–ix; reprinted in *Foundations of Cataloging: A Sourcebook,* ed. Michael Carpenter and Elaine Svenonius (Littleton: Colo.: Libraries Unlimited, 1985), p. 3–14.

2. Charles A. Cutter, *Rules for a Dictionary Catalog,* 4th ed. (Washington, D.C.: Government Printing Office, 1904) (1st ed., 1876).

3. Charles C. Jewett, *On the Construction of Catalogues of Libraries, and Their Publication by Means of Separate, Stereotyped Titles with Rules and Examples,* 2nd ed. (Washington, D.C.: Smithsonian Institution, 1853) (1st ed., 1852).

4. *Cataloguing Rules: Author and Title Entries,* English ed. (London: The Library Association, 1908); *Catalog Rules: Author and Title Entries,* American ed. (Chicago: American Library Association, 1908).

5. *Anglo-American Cataloging Rules. North American Text* (Chicago: American Library Association, 1967); *Anglo-American Cataloguing Rules. British Text* (London: The Library Association, 1967).

6. *Anglo-American Cataloguing Rules,* 2nd ed. (Chicago: American Library Association; London: The Library Association, 1978).

7. Biblioteca Apostolica Vaticana, *Norme per il catalogo degli stampati* (Cittá del Vaticano: Biblioteca Apostolica Vaticana, 1931).

8. Biblioteca Apostolica Vaticana, *Rules for the Catalog of Printed Books,* trans. Thomas J. Shanahan, Victor A. Schaefer, Constantin T. Vesselowsky, ed. Wyllis E. Wright (Chicago: American Library Association, 1948). Translation of: Biblioteca Apostolica Vaticana, *Norme per il catalogo degli stampati,* 2nd ed. (Cittá del Vaticano: Biblioteca Apostolica Vaticana, 1939).

9. American Library Association, Catalog Code Revision Committee, *A.L.A. Catalog Rules: Author and Title Entries,* prelim. American 2nd ed. (Chicago: American Library Association, 1941).

10. Andrew D. Osborne, "The Crisis in Cataloging, a Paper Read before the American Library Institute at the Harvard Faculty Club, June 21, 1941" ([Chicago]: American Library Institute, 1941); published in *Library Quarterly* 11, no. 4 (Oct. 1941): 393–411, and reprinted in *Foundations of Cataloging*, p. 92–103.

11. American Library Association, Division of Cataloging and Classification, *A.L.A. Cataloging Rules for Author and Title Entries*, 2nd ed., ed. Clara Beetle (Chicago: American Library Association, 1949).

12. Library of Congress, Descriptive Cataloging Division, *Rules for Descriptive Cataloging in the Library of Congress (Adopted by the American Library Association)* (Washington, D.C.: Library of Congress, 1949).

13. John Horner, *Cataloguing* (London: Association of Assistant Librarians, 1970), p. 72.

14. [Seymour Lubetzky], Library of Congress, Processing Dept., *Studies of Descriptive Cataloging: A Report to the Librarian of Congress by the Director of the Processing Department* (Washington, D.C.: Government Printing Office, 1946).

15. Seymour Lubetzky, *Cataloging Rules and Principles: A Critique of the A.L.A. Rules for Entry and a Proposed Design for Their Revision* (Washington, D.C.: Library of Congress, 1953; reprint, High Wycombe, England: Published for the College of Librarianship, Wales, by University Microfilms, 1970).

16. Lubetzky, *Cataloging Rules and Principles*, p. 36.

17. Paul S. Dunkin, *Cataloging U.S.A.* (Chicago: American Library Association, 1969), p. 28, citing Lubetzky's restatement of the principles in *Code of Cataloging Rules*, p. ix (see the following note).

18. Seymour Lubetzky, *Code of Cataloging Rules: Author and Title Entry: An Unfinished Draft for a New Edition of Cataloging Rules, Prepared for the Catalog Code Revision Committee*, with an explanatory commentary by Paul Dunkin (Chicago: American Library Association, 1960).

19. International Conference on Cataloguing Principles, *Statement of Principles Adopted at the International Conference on Cataloguing Principles, Paris, October 1961*, annotated ed. with commentary and examples, ed. Eva Verona (London: British Museum; International Federation of Library Associations (Committee on Cataloguing), 1971).

3

Musings on Cataloging and Information Science in Appreciation of Seymour Lubetzky

MICHÈLE V. CLOONAN

A catalog, to be most useful, must be made for the people who are to use it, and not for some theoretically ideal people contemplated by codes of rules.

—Edna D. Bullock, 1901[1]

The use of technology . . . is not an end in itself, but a means to an end. When, in an enthusiasm for technology, the end—that is, the objective of a pursuit—is lost sight of, the technology is miscarried.

—Seymour Lubetzky, 1998[2]

These remarks—written almost a century apart—reflect two themes that, as leitmotivs, continue to reappear in the discourses of library and information science (LIS) professionals: organizing information so that it is retrievable (and therefore useful) and harnessing technology to meet (library) users' needs. The organization and retrieval of information are the very core of our profession; how are these central activities carried out in our increasingly digital world?

Before attempting to answer this question, I must warn the reader that my musings have as their ultimate aim the recognition of the work of Seymour Lubetzky. This recognition will try to put his accomplishments into the context of the LIS field generally and not just with respect to cataloging. I hope to evaluate Lubetzky's approach to cataloging as it compares to other complementary areas of the LIS field.

Seymour Lubetzky has brought to the field of library and information science a philosopher's ability to construe a system of inquiry or demonstration. Lubetzky's subject of inquiry was the library catalog and cataloging rules, and he constructed a critique and analysis of then current beliefs (a few principles and many more rules) and how these beliefs came to be conceptualized and formulated. Lubetzky drew on the cataloging principles of Sir Anthony Panizzi of the British Library and Charles A. Cutter of the Boston Athenaeum, and also on a variety of rules, beginning with the 1908 *Catalog Rules: Author and Title Entries*.[3]

How did Seymour Lubetzky become a cataloging theorist?[4] Born in Zelwa, then Russia, later Poland, and now Belarus, Lubetzky became a primary- and secondary-school teacher after attending a teacher-training institute. Social and political conditions persuaded Lubetzky to immigrate to the States where he joined his siblings in Los Angeles. He earned a B.A. from UCLA and an M.A. from Berkeley. At these two University of California campuses, he studied French, German, music, and education, and also received a certificate in librarianship. Lubetzky's music and language training are reflected in his work: his writings combine the order and clarity of a musical scale with the close attention to the details of structure and development necessary to linguistics.

The subject of cataloging captivated Lubetzky even as a Berkeley student, where he studied it with Della J. Sisler. In characteristic fashion, Lubetzky "found her discussion of punctuation and capitalization practices essentially without reasons to back them."[5] It would be interesting to know how his former professor responded to his 1940 publication, "Capital Punishment for Catalogers?"[6] Noteworthy about this and other Lubetzky publications is that he draws his metaphors—and lessons—from the larger world of law, politics, and war.

For Seymour Lubetzky, a catalog was a system of principles in which every cataloging rule must be an offshoot of these principles. At the same time, Lubetzky's brand of philosophy was rooted in pragmatism—the doctrine that the meaning of a proposition lies in its practicable consequences. So when the new administration of the Library of Congress (under Archibald MacLeish) recruited Lubetzky in 1943 to examine the 1941 draft cataloging code and simplify the rules for cataloging description, it was probably for two reasons: (1) Lubetzky was already recognized for his ability to critique current cataloging practices; and (2) LC cataloging operations were in decline, with backlogs increasing and productivity decreasing. A logical scheme for descriptive cataloging should lead to more efficient cataloging practices, and to a triumph of both theory and function. There was no more suitable person to undertake this behemoth project than the independent-thinking Seymour Lubetzky.

The role of Lubetzky in the national information fabric might be compared to that of another important thinker: Vannevar Bush. At the same period in which Lubetzky was conceptualizing a new national cataloging code at the Library of Congress,[7] Bush was Director of the Office of Scientific Research and Development where he coordinated the activities of some 6,000 American scientists in applying science to warfare. (As an aside, just before Lubetzky went to the Library of Congress in 1943, he organized small-parts stock at a shipyard in Oakland as his contribution to the war effort.) After the war, in a pivotal article, "As We May Think," Bush urged scientists to turn their attention to the task of making information more accessible.[8] If the war years had extended mankind's physical powers, the postwar years should focus on the powers of the mind; and technology was a ready (and constantly evolving) tool.

Bush believed that records to be of use to science needed to be continuously extended (created, recorded), stored (preserved), and consulted (retrieved). He conceptualized many new technologies for the creation of records, and he also anticipated that the proliferation of records would be useless if they could not be retrieved. He discussed indexing in a general way, painting a future in which lawyers, for example, could easily access legal opinions and cases—and this in 1945! He intriguingly proposed that instead of accessing records through "the artificiality of systems of indexing . . . alphabetically or numerically," we should be able to access them the way in which our minds work: "by the association of thoughts, in accordance with some intricate web of trails carried by the cells of the brain."[9]

Bush and Lubetzky were complementary in their quests to make information easily accessible, but they were divergent in their approaches. Lubetzky, the humanist, looked to words, concepts, and logic in organizing information, while Bush, the scientist, conceptualized the end result with the same zeal with which Silicon Valley visionaries today see a technological solution for every problem just around the corner. Bush did not build a foundation or develop a set of basic assumptions on which an indexing system could be developed according to how the brain worked (if such a feat could have been possible). Rather, he began with a technology—a photoelectric cell and digital circuitry that could be used to search microfilm for specified patterns—and an optimism about science, and Big Science. In the end, Bush was perhaps a victim of that optimism.[10]

Research on Vannevar Bush by historian Colin Burke is now forcing scholars to examine Bush's contributions to information science in a new light. In the article "The Other Memex: The Tangled Career of Vannevar Bush's Information Machine, The Rapid Selector" and then later in a full-length book,[11] Burke demonstrates that Bush continued to push his indexing machines long after he knew that they would not work. (In fact, he used his formidable industry, foundation, and government connections to continue to raise money for the Memex, Comparator, and Rapid Selector.) Furthermore, Bush generally worked in isolation from—rather than in response to—the needs of librarianship and information science. Worse still, Bush failed to examine the principles behind indexing and retrieval when conceptualizing his Memex machine. Had he focused more on theoretical models for information retrieval and less on a particular technology, Bush might have developed a machine that worked.

Lubetzky espoused a more cautious approach to information retrieval that anticipated possible problems, while Bush was unquestionably overly optimistic. Bush saw potential outcomes and made conjectures about how we may reach them. Lubetzky began with principles of organization that were developed by Anthony Panizzi (who tried to organize information in a logical yet useful way) and Charles A. Cutter (who partially based his ideas on how he thought the library user might look for information).

The organization of and access to information continue to absorb our thinking in this digital age. But the landscape has become broader and more complex, and the players more diffuse. Today, professional librarians and archivists are only two of the many groups who organize information. As the network society grows, so does the number of players.

The Internet originated in the U.S. Defense Department's Advanced Research Projects Agency (DARPA). After Sputnik alarmed the American high-tech military establishment, DARPA designed a communications system invulnerable to nuclear attack.[12] The network that was formed,

ARPANET, went online in 1969. It was originally made available to research centers involved with the U.S. Defense Department. In the 1980s additional networks were established and operated by the National Science Foundation (ARPA-INTERNET), which were then opened up to other users. Of interest to us here, though, is that the structure of today's Internet is "a unique blending of military strategy, Big Science cooperation, and countercultural innovation."[13]

The technical, organizational, and cultural aspects of the World Wide Web (or Net) are the result not of a Janus, or Two Cultures, as articulated by C. P. Snow, but of many cultures, many visions, more in keeping with Aldous Huxley's perspective. The combination of these cultures is at times strange, even jarring to the traditionally trained bibliographer or cataloger. For example, instead of an index or catalog of the Web (a word Bush himself used to describe trails of thoughts carried by the brain), we have multiple search engines. These search engines are organized according to schemes (I dare not say principles!) that are opaque and usually proprietary. Therefore, even if they were constructed according to principles, we could not learn them.

There is no Lubetzky behind Infoseek or Alta Vista. And there is no Cutter either. Cutter's Objects—written more than 100 years ago—stated that the role of the catalog was:

1. To enable a person to find a book of which either
   (A) the author
   (B) the title > is known
   (C) the subject

2. To show what the library has
   (D) by a given author
   (E) on a given subject
   (F) in a given kind of literature

3. To assist in the choice of a book
   (G) as to its edition (bibliographically)
   (H) as to its character (literary or topical).

In an interesting twist on these objects, now there is a search engine that will lead to dead universal resource locators (URLs). So today we seem to have embraced as only one object to show what a library once had! This is perhaps an example of organizing information by novelty rather than by principle.

The word *Web* itself has a double meaning. A web is something that has interconnectedness, but it is also something that ensnares and tangles. And the language of the Web reflects this ambiguity: it is, by turns, straightforward, wacky, irreverent, or tasteless, reflecting traditional reference models, science fiction, counterculture, and perhaps, at times, trash. My favorite example is a search engine called Yahoo. Most people probably assume that a yahoo is merely a crude, brutish, or boorish creature. Thus, as a search engine moniker, the name is amusing (even reminiscent of Bush's description of physical versus mental power). But recall for a moment how Lemuel Gulliver described the Yahoos: "Their shape was very singular and deformed. . . . I never beheld in all my Travels so disagreeable an Animal, or one against which I naturally conceived so strong an Antipathy."[14]

Is this a small example of Two Cultures? Many cultures? Fractured cultures? Or one culture with many fibers or threads? Regardless, the visual image of a Yahoo, which Jonathan Swift artfully describes, is vivid, and to some even self-mocking. This is but a small example of the culture of the Web. It is a system that may permit universal access but it does so through stratification.

If we believe that the Web blends multiple backgrounds and perspectives, then it is time for librarians, archivists, and information specialists to make their visions known and felt. There is a place for principle and reason and we do not have to extend technological prowess at the expense of lucid thinking. To put it another way, search engine designers might do well to observe the law of parsimony, or Occam's Razor, to examine what is already known about searching behavior.

At a recent Getty Center symposium,[15] a representative from a Silicon Valley software company told the librarians in the audience that they had already lost control of the Internet and that the rules of cataloging impeded the creative, spontaneous, even ad hoc nature of the Web. But is it necessary to abandon creativity for a world of pure order and control? And would it ultimately be a "good" thing to try to rein in the power of the cyberworld? Should information be "controlled"? Can it be? Despite unfortunate terms coined by librarians such as *bibliographic control* and *nonbook cataloging,* the information professions are not out to inhibit creativity. On the contrary, art itself is based on certain conventions, such as musical scales or color theory. An architect would never champion pure design over the principles of engineering.[16]

Nor should we abandon the Web on such grounds. After all, digital information has its own standards and conventions. But the Internet must not be pure engineering; it must encompass the art of organization, or it will become a house of cards.

I would like to return to the two quotations with which I began. Edna Bullock's observation might today be revised to read, "The Internet, to be most useful, must be made for the people who are to use it." Lubetzky's observation, in his paper at the UCLA Symposium, is also fitting: "the use of technology . . . is not an end in itself, but a means to an end. When, in an enthusiasm for technology, the end—that is, the objective of a pursuit—is lost sight of, the technology is miscarried."

Aldous Huxley urges us to make the most of the different yet complementary insights of science and literature: "That the purified language of science, or the even more purified language of literature should ever be adequate to the givenness of the world and of our experience is impossible. . . . let us advance together, men of letters and men of science, further and further into the ever-expanding regions of the unknown."[17]

Or as Bertram C. Brookes put it: "The theoretical structure of a science is never complete or closed; every aspect of it remains always open, offering new problems."[18] The Web has provided us with more than new conceptual problems: it is altering how we think about information.

As philosophers, librarians, information scientists, and technologists, we should adhere to the rigorous methodology and principles that were developed by Panizzi and Cutter in the nineteenth century and Lubetzky in the twentieth. It is because of such clear foresight and thorough understanding of the needs of users that Seymour Lubetzky's work continues to demand our attention.

This chapter is an expansion of themes that I addressed only briefly in my welcoming remarks at the Lubetzky Symposium. I further developed them for a talk which I gave to the Los Angeles Chapter of the American Society for Information Science (LACASIS) on November 10, 1998, in honor of Seymour Lubetzky. The title of that talk was "From Fiber to Cyber and Back: Some Musings on Cataloging and Information Science in Appreciation of Seymour Lubetzky."

NOTES

1. Edna D. Bullock, "Practical Cataloging," *Public Libraries* 6 (1901): 136. Thanks to Professor Mary Niles Maack for bringing this article to my attention.

2. See Chapter 1, "The Vicissitudes of Ideology and Technology in Anglo-American Cataloging since Panizzi and a Prospective Reformation of the Catalog for the Next Century," by Seymour Lubetzky.

3. *Catalog Rules: Author and Title Entries,* comp. committees of the American Library Association and the (British) Library Association. American ed. (Chicago: American Library Association Publishing Board, 1908).

4. I have drawn on two sources here: my own "GSE&IS Celebrates a Centenarian on the Eve of the Millennium," *GSE&IS Forum* 2, no. 2 (Winter 1998): 8–9; and Michael Carpenter, "Seymour Lubetzky as a Teacher of Cataloging," in Carolynne Myall and Ruth C. Carter, eds., *Portraits in Cataloging and Classification: Theorists, Educators, and Practitioners of the Late Twentieth Century* (New York and London: The Haworth Press, 1998), p. 181–90.

5. Carpenter, "Seymour Lubetzky," p. 186.

6. Seymour Lubetzky, "Capital Punishment for Catalogers?" *Library Quarterly* 10, no. 3 (July 1940): 350–60.

7. [Seymour Lubetzky], Library of Congress, Processing Dept., *Studies of Descriptive Cataloging: A Report to the Librarian of Congress by the Director of the Processing Department* (Washington, D.C.: Government Printing Office, 1946).

8. Vannevar Bush, "As We May Think," *Atlantic Monthly* 176 (July 1945): 101–8.

9. Bush, "As We May Think," p. 106.

10. The contrast—even conflict—between the humanistic and scientific approaches was described by C. P. Snow in his *The Two Cultures* (New York: Cambridge University Press, 1961). One of the first critics to attack Snow's views was F. R. Leavis in his essay "Two Cultures? The Significance of Lord Snow" written in 1962 and reprinted in *Nor Shall My Sword: Discourses on Pluralism, Compassion and Social Hope* (London: Chatto & Windus, 1972), p. 39–74. Leavis comes across as excessively high-minded and supercilious; he misses the value of Snow's work. It took Aldous Huxley to do justice to the notion of the two cultures. In his *Literature and Science* (New

York: Harper & Row, 1963), he shows not only the divergent views of literature and science, but convergent and even complementary perspectives.

11. Colin Burke, "The Other Memex: The Tangled Career of Vannevar Bush's Information Machine, The Rapid Selector," *Journal of the American Society for Information Science* 43.10 (December 1992): 648–57, and his *Information and Secrecy: Vannevar Bush, Ultra, and the Other Memex* (Metuchen, N.J.: Scarecrow Press, 1994).

12. Paul Baran at Rand Corporation conceived of the idea. See Howard Rheingold, *The Virtual Community: Homesteading on the Electronic Frontier* (Reading, Mass.: Addison-Wesley, 1993).

13. Manuel Castells, The Rise of the Network Society, vol. 1 of *The Information Age: Economy, Society and Culture* (Oxford, U.K.: Blackwell, 1996), p. 351.

14. Jonathan Swift, *Gulliver's Travels: An Authoritative Text,* 2nd ed. (New York: W. W. Norton, 1970), p. 193.

15. "Communicating Culture," The Getty Center Institute Conference, held at the Getty Center, Los Angeles, October 22–23, 1998.

16. The Babylonian *Code of Hammurabi* levied severe penalties against architects whose buildings failed. How might King Hammurabi deal with today's inadequate search engines? By cutting off the fingers of their designers?

17. Huxley, *Literature and Science,* p. 118.

18. Bertram C. Brookes, "The Foundations of Information Science. Part I. Philosophical Aspects," *Journal of Information Science* 2.3/4 (October 1980): 125.

Current Research
in Cataloging

4

Modeling Relevance in Art History

SARA SHATFORD LAYNE

This chapter briefly describes the methodology developed for my dissertation and summarizes some of the results.

I looked at the problem of matching art historians' information needs with original art works, representations of art works, and primary materials that might prove useful to those art historians in their research. I called these materials, as a group, "Documents" (see Figure 1). In this chapter I am going to address the aspect of my dissertation that dealt with matching the art historian's information needs with original art works and representations of art works. From this point on, *art works* will include both original art works and representations of those works.

My idea was if I could figure out which attributes of art works cause them to be of interest to art historians, or, in other words, which attributes of art works determine relevance, and if I could determine how often a given attribute determines relevance, then that knowledge could guide decisions in cataloging and indexing art works, as well as in system design. This may sound a little abstract and even obscure, but an example will illustrate that this idea is actually a relatively simple concept. Picture a tenth-century mosaic depicting a peacock. Imagine an art historian researching the symbolism of peacocks in art. It is pretty clear

FIGURE 1 Documents

Art Works
    Original
    Represented Works
        (i.e., Reproductions and Representations of Art Works)
Primary Resources
    Images
        (e.g., Photographs, Home Movies)
    Text
        Unpublished
            (e.g., Archives)
        Published
            (e.g., Science Fiction)

that the art historian would be interested in the tenth-century mosaic, and that which would render the mosaic interesting to the art historian is that it depicts a peacock, not that it is a mosaic or is created in the tenth century. In other words, it is the subject of the mosaic—the subject *attribute* of the mosaic—that determines its relevance to the art historian's research. If the art historian were researching the symbolism of peacocks in the tenth century, then both the subject attribute and the date attribute would determine the relevance of this art work to the art historian's research.

The first task, then, was to figure out what art historians are studying; the second, to figure out what the attributes of art works are; the third, to figure out how to match up the two; and the fourth and final, to analyze the data. This sounds fairly simple, but many complexities were involved.

To figure out what art historians are studying, I looked at published research in art history, specifically at abstracts of articles. Published research was examined, rather than looking at how art historians query databases, because any examination of actual use of databases for art works would be greatly affected by the generally limited nature of those databases. That is, in a study of actual queries, one might find that certain kinds of access were not used—but if those kinds of access were not provided by the particular system I would simply be reinforcing the status quo, not identifying what kinds of access *should* exist.

The subject of an art historian's published research or article is not precisely equivalent to what that art historian studied to produce that published article. In other words, the subject of an art historian's research is not equivalent to the query that art historian would have posed to an ideal system to obtain relevant art works. My belief was (and is), however, that the query *could* be derived from the subject of the research. I remember that in beginning reference class we were taught that if you could elicit from someone a description of his or her research, you would be better able to help him or her find material relevant to that research. Looking at published research is roughly equivalent to listening to the reference patron describe his or her research.

In the peacock example, the subject of the art historian's research is the symbolism of peacocks in art. That does not mean that he or she needs to view works of art about the *symbolism* of peacocks; it means that he or she needs to view works of art that *depict* peacocks. The term I use to describe what the art historian studies, as different from the subject of the research, is "Research Focus" (see Figure 2). Research focus is divided into three components: the object of the research, the purpose of the research, and the emphasis of the research. In the peacock example, the object component of the research focus consisted of art works with a given attribute (namely, subject); the purpose component was deciphering symbolism, or, in other words, analysis of meaning; and the emphasis component was a group of art works with a common attribute.

To obtain data on the components of the research focus in art history, the technique of content analysis was used on a random sample of 239 abstracts taken from RILA *(Répertoire international de la littérature de l'art),* which indexes and abstracts the literature of art.[1] These

FIGURE 2   Research Focus

Object
   Person(s)
      Attributes
         (e.g., Name; Nationality)
   Art Work(s)
      Attributes
         (e.g., Artist; Material or Medium)
Purpose
      (e.g., Attribution; Analysis of Meaning)
Emphasis
      (e.g., on one or more art works with proper names;
      on a group of persons with common attributes)

---

abstracts represented articles published between 1977 and 1988, 85 percent of which appeared in journals and 15 percent in monographic collections. These and other details about the source articles may be seen in Figure 3.

This took care of the first part of what I set out to do, figuring out what art historians are studying. For the second part—figuring out the attributes of art works—I looked at a variety of sources, including various classification schemes and vocabularies as well as a preliminary analysis of a small sample of article abstracts. Once I had identified and categorized the attributes of art works, I was ready for the third part of my task.

The third part was to figure out how to match what art historians are studying with the attributes of art works, or, in other words, to develop a relevance model. The relevance model I developed uses the component parts of the research focus to establish the circumstances under which the various attributes of art works are determinants of relevance for art history research. Rather than describe the details of the relevance

FIGURE 3 Sources of Articles

Abstracted: 1980–1989
Published: 1977–1988

From journals: 202 (85%)
From monographic collections: 37 (15%)

Sources supplying
    4 to 13 articles each: 11
    2 or 3 articles each: 33
    1 article each: 90

Sources classified using the Library of Congress
    N *Classification* (Arts) schedule: 183 (77%)
    Other LCC schedules: 56 (23%)

Categorized by RILA as:
    Renaissance to Modern periods (i.e., fifteenth century to 1945): 77%
    General or Medieval: 23%

    Fine arts: 60% (approximate)
    Applied arts: 40% (approximate)

model, the remainder of this chapter is about the fourth part of my task, the analysis of the data and some of its implications.

I used the data to establish the percentages of research for which a given art work attribute is a determinant of relevance. Figure 4 lists the attributes in descending order of frequency and shows what percentage of the research each attribute is a strong attribute of relevance. Here we see some relationship between my research and Seymour Lubetzky's contributions to cataloging theory. Lubetzky's ideas are so fundamental to my understanding of cataloging, and I take them for granted to such a degree, that I actually had not been conscious of this relationship until I was preparing for this report. Lubetzky, almost forty years ago, described the second objective for the catalog as "to relate and display together the editions which a library has of a given work and the works

FIGURE 4   Art Work Attributes as Determinants of Relevance

Attribute	Strong Determinants of Relevance
Owner, etc.-Name	144 (60%)
Artist or Creator-Name	143 (60%)
Subject-of-Specific-Person-Name	140 (59%)
Kind of Work	130 (51%)
Date	111 (46%)
Subject (other than real persons associated with Art works, and Technique or material as a subject)	101 (42%)
Place	91 (38%)
Owner, etc.-Attribute	67 (28%)
Artist, etc.-Attribute	66 (28%)
Subject-of-Generic-Person-Attribute	60 (25%)
Title-proper name	62 (26%)
Style	59 (25%)
Technique or Material	50 (21%)
Related Literary Work	35 (15%)
Title-no proper name	25 (10%)
Subject-of-Technique or Material	14 (6%)

which it has of a given author."[2] My research quantifies how often, for art historians, this objective is important, assuming that the "author" in the case of art works is the artist or other creator, and that editions of the work encompass representations of a given work of art. And in Figure 4 we see how important these objectives are. In 60 percent of art history research, "Artist or Creator" (identified by name) is a strong determinant of relevance. Regarding editions of a work, by adding the two attributes Title-proper name and Title-no proper name (these were mutually exclusive categories in the data analysis), we see that for 36 percent of research the title of a specific work is a strong determinant of relevance. I should point out here that by "title" I mean what many people mean by "main entry"—that is, an identifier for the work that consists of an artist's name, when appropriate, together with the title, or uniform title, for the work.

As part of the research, I also looked at how often people were identified, not by a proper name, but by one or more attributes (for example, twentieth-century Russian painters). I found that roughly one-quarter of the research conducted by art historians would benefit from having access to art works through the attributes, rather than through the specific names, of persons. This has implications for system design and authority control. It would be nice if a researcher could query a system for all the works of twentieth-century Russian painters, rather than having to compile a list of such painters and search for each one individually.

Looking again at Figure 4, one can see four principal attributes (besides those already mentioned) that have high frequencies of occurrence: Kind of Work, Date, Subject, and Place. Style, Technique or Material, and Related Literary Work have lower frequencies of occurrence.

Kind of Work includes what librarians currently call genre or form. Examples of Kind of Work in my sample ranged from "cathedrals" to "masks" to "working drawings." The frequency with which this attribute determines relevance supports the development of controlled vocabularies for it, and also, in my opinion, for systems to make clear to researchers the distinction between, for example, records for art works that *are* portraits, and records for works that *depict* or are *about* portraits, as, for instance, photographs of room interiors that contain portraits, or books that discuss the painting of portraits.

Date is another attribute that frequently determines relevance of art works. This result supports the indexing of this attribute, and perhaps supports more complex indexing than some systems now provide. For example, a system should be able to match a query for eighteenth-century paintings with an art work dated 1765.

Subject is a determinant of relevance for art works for nearly half of research in art history. Subject is one of the most problematic attributes to index. I have thought about the subject attribute of art works quite a bit and believe a useful way to look at the subject or subjects of an art work is to break down the subject into *of* and *about*.[3] For instance, an art work might be *of* a grave digger and *about* death. Furthermore, what an art work is *of* may be described in both generic and specific terms. For example, an art work depicting the prophet Elisha is, *generically*, of a prophet, while, at the same time, *specifically* of Elisha. I did attempt in my research to identify which subject categories it would be most useful to index and came to the tentative conclusion that it would serve more researchers to index Of than to index About, but that within the Of category it would be useful to index both generic and specific Of-ness. This is an area, however, where more research must be conducted.

Place—place of location or creation, rather than place depicted (which would be subject)—also occurs fairly frequently as a determinant of relevance. The place names occurring in my sample ranged from parts of individual buildings (the Great Hall, Windsor Castle) to continents (North America). My results support the indexing of place names and the need for indexing them in some type of hierarchical structure that would permit a researcher to find art works created or located in places of varying size. For example, an art historian should be able to find art works created or located in Paris, in France, or even in Europe.

Style is a very problematic attribute to index, as universally accepted definitions of particular styles are difficult to achieve, and art historians may by no means agree that a given art work is in a particular style. Although style is an attribute that determines relevance, it is a sufficiently subjective attribute that art historians might prefer to have access to art works through less subjective attributes, such as date and place, and make the style determination themselves. It seems possible that many style terms can be at least approximately expressed in terms of date and place—for example, "Elizabethan" corresponds approximately to sixteenth-century England. This is a topic for future research with a larger sample than mine.

The importance of the title, or, more accurately, the identifier, for a particular work has already been mentioned as a determining attribute of relevance; my research can be taken as supporting the creation of authority records for specific art works, both named and unnamed. The art librarians, through the Art Libraries Society of North America (ARLIS/NA) Cataloging Advisory Committee, are currently working with the Library of Congress on the problems of devising uniform titles for art works.

Technique or Material is a determinant of relevance for approximately one-quarter of art history research, which I think makes it worthwhile to index.

An obvious example of the Related Literary Work attribute, because it may not be self-evident, would be prints designed to illustrate Jonathan Swift's *Tale of a Tub*—in this case, Swift's *Tale of a Tub* is a Related Literary Work. A Related Literary Work is a determinant of relevance for a relatively small percentage—approximately 15 percent—of art history research. This may be more a measure of the presence of the attribute, however, for not all art works *have* related literary works, than it is a measure of how often, when that attribute is present, it is a determinant of relevance. If it is a measure of its presence, we might say that it is definitely worth indexing when it is there, for it is a determinant of relevance.

The question might be asked—did I find any terms in my sample that didn't fit into the attribute categories on this list? The answer is yes, I did—such terms occurred in just 7 percent of my sample. In other words, 93 percent of research would be completely served by indexing the attributes on this list; only 7 percent would be incompletely served. I looked at the nonconforming terms and categorized them, identifying five new attributes: Formal Elements, Shape, Color, Physical Condition, and Marks. Of these, a striking characteristic of four of them (all except physical condition) is that they are very difficult and time-consuming to index by traditional, textual means, but that they are ideally suited to automated, computer-aided identification, because they involve purely visual matching. Given the low incidence of these attributes as determinants of relevance, and the difficulties they pose for human indexers, I suggest that indexing these attributes is best left to automated techniques.

In addition to looking at the individual frequencies with which a given attribute was a determinant of relevance, I performed, with the help of a statistician, co-occurrence analyses of the art work attributes. Co-occurrence analyses tell us when the presence or absence of a particular attribute suggests that another attribute will also be present or absent. I thought it would be helpful for vocabulary and system design to know which attributes were likely to co-occur (or unlikely to co-occur) with each other.

The co-occurrence analyses suggest that six principal patterns might be desirable for access to art works. These patterns, in descending order of frequency, are access by:

1. people attributes, including name as an attribute;
2. kind of work, subdivided or qualified by date or place;
3. subject or related literary work;
4. titles (i.e., main entries) of specific works;
5. style;
6. technique or material.

It would be useful to pay attention to these patterns when designing information retrieval systems for art works. These patterns, for example, could guide in selecting names and content of indexes for a system; they could also suggest initial choices that could be offered in a menu-driven system.

I would like to conclude with something that Gregory Tschann, writing about the Getty's *Categories for the Description of Works of Art,* said: "There is a high cost to pay for indexing many fields, both in terms of the cataloging effort necessary to parse the data and the system overhead incurred by extensive indexing. No research on 'researching' exists to determine what access points will be needed to do adequate retrievals."[4] My dissertation was an attempt to provide some of this research on researching.

NOTES

1. *Répertoire international de la littérature de l'art: RILA = International Repertory of the Literature of Art,* 15 vols. (New York: College Art Association of America, 1975–1989).

2. Seymour Lubetzky, *Code of Cataloging Rules: Author and Title Entry: An Unfinished Draft for a New Edition of Cataloging Rules, Prepared for the Catalog Code Revision Committee,* with an explanatory commentary by Paul Dunkin (Chicago: American Library Association, 1960), p. ix.

3. Sara Shatford, "Analyzing the Subject of a Picture: A Theoretical Approach," *Cataloging & Classification Quarterly* 6, no. 3 (Spring 1986): 39–62.

4. Gregory Tschann, "Categories in Context: Implementation Issues regarding the *AITF Categories for the Description of Works of Art,*" *Visual Resources* 11, no. 3/4 (1996): 307.

5

Creating Efficient and Systematic Catalogs

ALLYSON CARLYLE

The intellectual challenge stimulated by the study of descriptive cataloging is matched by few topics in library and information science. As a student entering library school at UCLA in 1982, I had no idea that cataloging would provide such a rich area of study. I was, however, quickly enlightened, and my life changed as a result. Seymour Lubetzky was largely responsible for this change because his work, which provided the conceptual foundation of the study of descriptive cataloging in this century, fascinated me first. I was fortunate to have been introduced to descriptive cataloging by Betty Baughman, who worked with Seymour Lubetzky in developing the cataloging courses at UCLA. The combination of her excellent teaching and the challenges posed by Lubetzky's analysis of cataloging problems drew me and my research to the heart of descriptive cataloging.

Central to Lubetzky's thought is the notion of a catalog as "a systematically designed instrument in which all entries, as component parts, must be properly integrated."[1] One important means by which a catalog becomes such an instrument is in meeting the second objective of the catalog. The second objective, most clearly articulated by Lubetzky in his *Code of Cataloging Rules,* states that a catalog must "relate and display together the editions which a library has of a given work and the works which it has of a given author."[2]

My research has as its focus the second objective, in particular the organization of author and work records in online catalogs. My dissertation examines the effect of various system features on the collocation of author and work records in online catalogs.[3] "Fulfilling the Second Objective in the Online Catalog" investigates how codes of filing rules and Barbara Tillett's bibliographic relationship taxonomy may be used to help organize author and work records more effectively in online catalogs.[4] "The Role of Classification in the Creation of Author and Work Displays in Online Catalogues" investigates the methods by which library classification schemes have organized author and work records.[5] Current research looks at the characteristics people use for grouping the editions and works related to a particular work.[6]

Ordering Author and Work Records

Computerization has vastly expanded the catalog's power to retrieve records. It has, at the same time, confounded catalog designers' attempts to create sensible displays. In my search for a dissertation topic, I was intrigued that no study had ever been conducted to determine how well a catalog of any kind fulfilled the second objective. I also suspected that the computerization of catalogs had an effect on the ability of catalogs to fulfill the second objective. As a result, I decided that my dissertation research would consist of a survey of online catalogs posing the question: what is the effect of online catalog features on the collocation of author and work records in online catalogs?

Several measures were used to analyze the effect of online catalog system features on collocation in online catalogs. Five worst-case authors (Homer, William James, H.D., Alice Walker, and Peter Gray) were searched in eighteen sample online catalogs using author commands available in those catalogs. Five worst-case works (John Milton's *Paradise Lost*, Charles Dickens's *A Christmas Carol*, James Joyce's *Ulysses*, William Shakespeare's *Sonnets*, and Sir Thomas More's *Utopia*) were searched in the same catalogs using title commands. The worst-case method was used because worst cases were seen as more likely to bring out the weaknesses of online catalogs than a random sample of searches would.

Dependent variables to measure the collocation of author and work records included: number of interruptions of author and record sets, number of irrelevant intervening records retrieved, and precision. Independent variables representing system features analyzed for their effects on collocation included match type (character string versus keyword) and catalog size (large, medium, or small).

The authors and works selected for sample searches, previously mentioned, were examples of worst cases. Worst cases were defined as authors and works that had many records in online catalogs and that were represented by a variety of record types. Sample catalogs were selected based on catalog vendor (major vendors were selected), availability via Internet, size (three sizes of catalog per vendor were selected: small, medium, and large), and collection characteristics (at least 75 percent of retrospective conversion to online catalog complete; English language, general library collection; located in the United States).

Selected Results and Discussion

Descriptive statistics were used to analyze the data collected in this study because the selection of worst-case searches and sample catalogs was not random. Because sample sizes were relatively small and many of the standard deviations were large, the median was reported instead of the mean.

Match type, that is, left-to-right phrase matching, here called character-string matching, versus keyword matching, was investigated for its effect on collocation. Character-string matches performed better than keyword matches for most searches. When author searches were measured using number of interruptions, the results were dramatic (see Figures 1 through 3). Only 10 percent of character-string matches had three or more interruptions. The median number of interruptions for keyword matches (3.5) was greater than the median for character-string matches (2.0). That most character-string matches had two or fewer interruptions indicated that in most cases character-string matches accomplished the goal of collocating author record sets.

The effect of match type on number of interruptions in work record sets was less clear, although character-string matches still performed better than keyword matches (see Figures 4 through 6). Seventy percent of character-string matches for work record sets had three or more interruptions, as opposed to 83 percent of keyword matches. The median

FIGURE 1   Match Type (Authors): Number of Interruptions

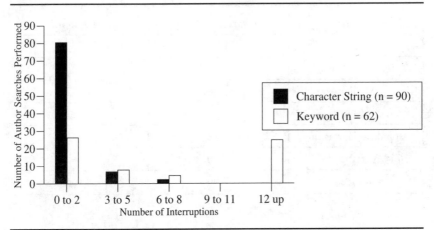

FIGURE 2   Distribution of Match Type (Authors): Number of Interruptions

Interrupts	Character-String Searches n = 90	Percent	Keyword Searches n = 62	Percent
0 to 2	81	90%	26	42%
3 to 5	7	8%	8	13%
6 to 8	2	2%	4	6%
9 to 11	0	0%	0	0%
12 up	0	0%	24	39%

number of interruptions for character-string matches was four and for keyword, it was five.

These results were not unexpected, particularly with respect to author record sets. Character-string matches matched a search string in a single field. Most character-string matches arranged records with identical author headings together, ensuring collocation of author record sets. Although author commands with character-string matches were available in every catalog surveyed, author commands with keyword

FIGURE 3   Statistics for Match Type (Authors): Number of Interruptions

Statistic	Character String	Keyword
Mean	1.71	17.15
Standard Error	.12	2.91
Median	2.00	3.50
Mode	2.00	2.00
Standard Deviation	1.18	22.94
Variance	1.40	526.03
Range	7.00	110.00

FIGURE 4   Match Type (Works): Number of Interruptions

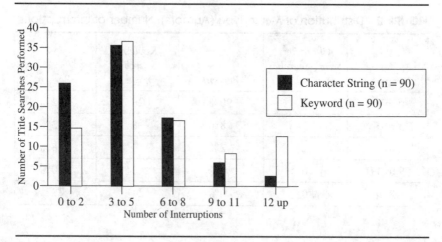

matches were not. This was perhaps because systems designers assumed the superiority of character-string matches for searching for individual authors. The results of this research support such an assumption.

The finding that character-string matches performed as poorly as keyword matches in collocating worst-case work record sets was somewhat unexpected. Because uniform titles for works are not required in AACR2, however, it was not surprising that work records did not collo-

FIGURE 5 Distribution of Match Type (Works): Number of Interruptions

Interrupts	Character-String Searches n = 90	Percent	Keyword Searches n = 90	Percent
0 to 2	27	30%	15	17%
3 to 5	36	40%	37	41%
6 to 8	18	20%	17	19%
9 to 11	6	7%	8	9%
12 up	3	3%	13	14%

FIGURE 6 Statistics for Match Type (Works): Number of Interruptions

Statistic	Character String	Keyword
Mean	4.67	6.49
Standard Error	0.36	0.60
Median	4.00	5.00
Mode	2.00	3.00
Standard Deviation	3.42	5.73
Variance	11.66	32.81
Range	19.00	36.00

cate well. Also, a work is, by definition, determined by the contents of two fields, an author and a title field, as opposed to an author, which is determined by the contents of a single field, an author field. The level of complexity engendered by the additional field, the title field, may itself have had an effect on record arrangement. This variable (record structure) was not studied. What was unexpected was that character-string matches differed so little from keyword matches in achieving collocation, especially considering that keyword matches often arranged records in essentially random (record number) order, and character-string title matches almost always arranged records in alphabetical order by title.

Catalogs searched were representative of catalog databases of different sizes. Small catalogs contained fewer than 299,999 bibliographic records, medium catalogs contained between 300,000 and 999,999 bibliographic records, and large catalogs contained more than 1,000,000 records.

Catalog size had a much smaller effect on collocation of author and work records than may have been expected; only about half of the results in the study showed an impact. Catalog size had the smallest effect on collocation of author record sets. Measured by the number of irrelevant records intervening in an author work set (number of irrelevant intervening records), very little effect was seen (see Figures 7 through 9). Although catalog size had some effect on the collocation of work record sets, when measured by precision, that effect was negligible (as shown in Figures 10 through 12).

The finding that catalog size had an effect on collocation only in about half the searches performed was surprising for two reasons. First, two of the measures used in the study, number of interruptions and number of irrelevant intervening records, were directly related to the number of records retrieved. One would expect that increasing numbers of records would be retrieved in small, medium, and large catalogs, respectively, and that measures based on record numbers would reflect that increase. It is also reasonable to expect that number of interruptions would increase as number of records retrieved increases, and that precision would be lower in a large catalog search than in a small catalog search.

That author record sets were little affected by catalog size was perhaps not so surprising when examining the performance of the system variables. For author searches, the variables that determined collocation most strongly were those associated with match type; character-string matches collocated author records more successfully than did keyword matches. Because catalogs of all sizes had character-string and keyword matches, one might predict that catalog size would not be an important factor.

The finding that catalog size did not have a powerful influence on collocation has implications for catalog maintenance and cataloging policies in small and medium-sized catalogs. Cataloging folklore purports collocation to be better in smaller catalogs because not so many records exist to interrupt a related record set. For example, AACR2 Rule 1.0D, which provides catalogs options for three different levels of description, and Rule 25.1A, which allows catalogers the option not to

FIGURE 7 Catalog Size (Authors): Number of Irrelevant Intervening Records

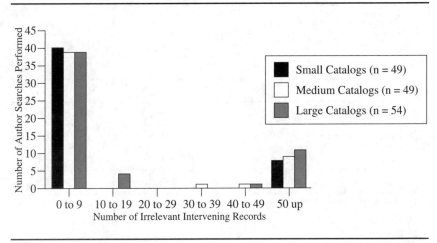

FIGURE 8 Distribution of Catalog Size (Authors): Number of Irrelevant Intervening Records

Intervening Records	Small	Percent	Medium	Percent	Large	Percent
0–9	40	84%	38	78%	38	70%
10–19	0	0%	0	0%	4	7%
20–29	0	0%	0	0%	0	0%
30–39	0	0%	1	2%	0	0%
40–49	0	0%	1	2%	1	2%
50 up	8	16%	9	18%	11	20%

use uniform titles, are evidence that smaller catalogs have been seen as having different requirements from larger catalogs. The findings of this research indicate that this assumption may be incorrect. Smaller catalogs may not be exempt from collocation problems, particularly for worst cases. They may require use of uniform author names and uniform titles as much as a larger catalog.

FIGURE 9   Statistics for Catalog Size (Authors): Number of Irrelevant Intervening Records

Statistic	Small	Medium	Large
Mean	26.96	84.98	187.46
Standard Error	10.10	31.42	65.08
Median	0.00	0.00	0.00
Mode	0.00	0.00	0.00
Standard Deviation	70.69	219.93	478.24
Variance	4,996.91	48,369.94	228,717.61
Range	366.00	956.00	2,101.00

FIGURE 10   Catalog Size (Works): Precision

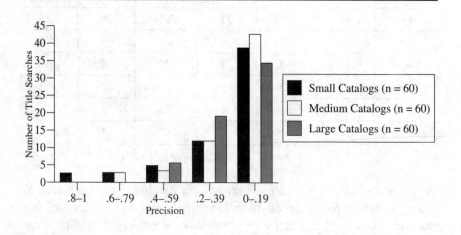

FIGURE 11 Distribution of Catalog Size (Works): Precision

Precision	Small	Percent	Medium	Percent	Large	Percent
.8–1	2	3%	0	0%	0	0%
.6–.79	2	3%	2	3%	0	0%
.4–.59	5	8%	3	5%	6	10%
.2–.39	13	22%	13	22%	20	33%
0–.19	38	63%	42	70%	34	57%

FIGURE 12 Statistics for Catalog Size (Works): Precision

Statistic	Small	Medium	Large
Mean	.22	.17	.19
Standard Error	.03	.02	.02
Median	.14	.12	.17
Mode	.17	.13	.17
Standard Deviation	.22	.16	.14
Variance	.05	.03	.02
Range	.99	.74	.51

Organizing Author and Work Records into Usable Displays

A study of filing rules as schemes for display came about as a result of both my dissertation research and Lubetzky's perception of the importance of the catalog as a "systematically designed instrument." What followed from this interaction is the research described in this section.

Filing Rules as Schemes for Display

Catalog displays as constructed by codes of filing rules are frequently highly organized, consisting of a variety of categories or groups of similar records. A historical analysis of codes of filing rules discovered the following common categories:

Work categories:

- Editions of the work in the original language,
- Analytics, that is, editions of the work contained within collections,
- Translations,
- Special classes of materials, including selections and manuscripts,
- Works about the work.

Author categories:

- Complete works,
- Selected works,
- Selections from a single work or from various works,
- Single works,
- Spurious and doubtful works,
- Works about the author.

While these categories may be used to create systematic displays in online catalogs, they fall short with respect to works, particularly when viewed in the light of Tillett's bibliographic relationship theory.[7] They do not, for instance, clearly distinguish or identify works related to a work, nor do they clearly distinguish or identify sequential relationships.

Tillett's Taxonomy of Bibliographic Relationships as a Scheme for Display

Tillett's taxonomy of bibliographic relationships[8] and Smiraglia's refinement of the derivative relationship[9] were analyzed for their potential contribution to the creation of systematic displays of work records in the catalog. The analysis suggested the following interpretation of the bibliographic relationships taxonomy to be used as a basis of a scheme for display organization:

- equivalence relationships, including:
    - equivalent texts, which share identical content and authorship,
    - near equivalents, which in addition to identical content and authorship, share other characteristics as well;
- derivative relationships, including:
    - revisions,
    - adaptations,
    - translations,
    - extractions,
    - amplifications;
- whole-part relationships;
- sequential relationships;
- descriptive relationships;
- shared characteristic relationships.

Using this scheme as a basis for online catalog work displays also has limitations, particularly the lack of a distinction between derivations whose intellectual or artistic content are close to the original edition and those whose intellectual or artistic content are not.

A Relationship-Based, Organized Scheme for Display of Author and Work Records

Analysis of the strengths of the filing rules scheme and the bibliographic relationships scheme led to the proposal of a new, organized scheme for display of author and works records in online catalogs based on relationships among items. The proposed scheme also incorporated records that could be retrieved in keyword searching that might or might not be related to the author or work searched, including records for items that might be only peripherally related to them (see Figures 13 and 14).

Using Classification in Author and Work Displays in Online Catalogs

Other organizational schemes that could be used to improve online catalog displays for author and work records are library classifications. Library classification schemes such as the Universal Decimal Classification

FIGURE 13 An Organized Display for Works

WORK NAME/AUTHOR NAME

Editions

- Books
- Recordings
- Large print, Braille, . . .
- [*work name*] published with other works

- Revisions, updated editions
- Translations

- Parts, selections, . . .

Adaptations and Related Works

- Abridgements, simplified versions, summaries
- Sequels, supplements
- Videos, motion pictures
- Musical versions
- Pictures or other images
- Multimedia, computer versions
- Indexes, concordances
- Miscellaneous

Works about [*work name*]

Items probably related to [*work name*]

Items that may or may not be related to [*work name*]

Other works by [*author name*]

(UDC), the Library of Congress Classification (LCC), and the Dewey Decimal Classification (DDC) organize authors and works associated with many items into specific classes, each with its own notation. In this research I analyzed the types of classes used in selected religion and literature schedules and in auxiliary tables in the UDC, the LCC, and the DDC.

Classes identified correspond closely to the types of groupings created by the codes of catalog filing rules. Commonly occurring classes for authors in the classification schemes included:

- complete works of the author,
- partial collections or selected works,
- individual works,
- biographies, criticism, concordances, etc.

FIGURE 14 An Organized Display for Authors

AUTHOR NAME

Single Works

- *Work names A–H*
- *Work names I–O*
- *Work names P–Z*

Collected Works

Selections from [*author name*]'s works

Spurious and doubtful works

Works about [*author name*]

Items probably related to [*author name*]

Items that may or may not be related to [*author name*]

Works by the same/related author: [*author name 2*]

Commonly occurring classes for works in the classification schemes included:

- editions in the original language, sometimes including groups for early versions, translations, annotated editions, and sequels;
- translated editions, sometimes including a special group for bilingual editions;
- auxiliary materials, including concordances, indexes, dictionaries, sources;
- parts or selections;
- adaptations, paraphrases;
- works about the work, including history, commentary, criticism, etc.

Classification numbers, possibly in combination with book numbers such as Cutter numbers, which further refine the groupings of authors and works on the shelf, might be used to create summary or grouped author and work displays automatically in online catalogs. Further research is necessary to determine whether or not automatic grouping would organize records successfully.

User Categorization
of Works

The design of online information systems, including online catalogs, should respond effectively to user needs and searching behavior. The last research project I review here investigated how people organize items related to a work. In this research project, fifty study participants were solicited in a shopping mall in Akron, Ohio, and asked to divide forty-seven editions and works related to Charles Dickens's *A Christmas Carol* into groups. Items in the study included hardcover and paperback versions, translations, children's versions, including picture-book versions, videorecordings of motion pictures and animated film versions, sound recordings, a trivia book, and an Advent calendar. Participants were asked to sort the items into groups based on their similarity to each other and the ability of the groups to help the participants find the items at a later time. Any number of groups were allowed, so long as it was more than one. When participants were finished with the sorting task, they were asked to name and describe in writing each of the groups they had created. The project produced two types of data: written descriptions and grouping data.

Written descriptions were analyzed using content analysis to discover the types of characteristics that were used to sort items in the study. Eleven types of characteristics were discovered. In the following list, types of characteristics are listed with sample participant descriptions in parentheses after each type.

1. physical format (hardback books, VCR tapes, little-kid tapes)
2. audience (youth, sight-impaired, grown-up people, piano players)
3. content description (play, more involved plots with more details, short version)
4. pictorial elements (animated, cartoon pictorial, had a man's face on the front, color art work, dull covers)
5. usage (could be read by small group for presentation, theater, for relaxation, fun, dull)
6. language (foreign-language, Spanish, non-English)
7. physical characteristics (medium-size, largest books, thick hard bind)
8. content age, integrity (unabridged, abbreviated versions, classic, original text-line)

9. textual characteristics (big-print, book [*sic*] that say Scrooge on them)
10. creator, performer (produced other than Charles Dickens, Disney-type story, adapted by other author's take from original)
11. "odds and ends" (alone, miscellaneous, other)

The grouping data were analyzed using cluster analysis (this part of the study has not yet been published). Preliminary analysis indicated the common groups listed:

- audios (cassettes and CDs),
- children's videos,
- adult videos,
- large-format paperbacks,
- small-format paperbacks,
- foreign-language materials,
- adult hardcover materials,
- illustrated hardcover materials (children's),
- trivia book,
- picture-book versions with lots of text,
- picture-book versions with not much text,
- activity versions (piano book, Advent calendar),
- item about *A Christmas Carol*.

This research is exploratory; the findings indicate possible types of groups and characteristics that may be useful for organizing online catalog displays. Every work is unique, and the group of editions and works about a particular work is equally as unique and individual. Further research using different works, and different types of works, for example, nonliterary works, is necessary to make generalizations regarding what groups and types of characteristics are commonly associated with people's perceptions of works. In addition, further research is required to determine the impact of grouping in online catalog displays on user searching, and whether or not grouping based on user categories is more effective than grouping based purely on relationships among items, such as that suggested by the filing rules and bibliographic relationships taxonomy analysis.

Conclusion

The extent to which a library catalog fulfills the second objective affects cataloger users every day. In my doctoral program at UCLA, I supported myself by working as a librarian at the Beverly Hills Public Library. One day at the information desk I received a long-distance telephone call from a woman in Arizona who was looking for an edition of *The Haunted Pool* by George Sand. She had telephoned four libraries in two states and reported that none of these libraries had an edition of the work she was seeking. My cataloging experience told me that this was unlikely, so I carefully browsed the titles by Sand in the Beverly Hills catalog and found several records for editions entitled *The Devil's Pool*. After looking at a machine-readable cataloging (MARC) record for one of these editions, I explained to her that the work she was seeking, *La mare au diable*, was most often translated into English under the title *The Devil's Pool*, and that she should telephone her own public library again and ask for this title instead of the title *The Haunted Pool*.

It should not take five telephone calls to libraries in two states and a cataloger at the information desk for a patron to find an edition of a work held commonly in American libraries. The catalog should be, as the Paris Principles state, "an efficient instrument for ascertaining . . . which works by a particular author and which editions of a particular work are in the library." It should not be a roadblock, preventing users and librarians alike from finding the items they seek. Lubetzky's life-work was to make library catalogs efficient and systematically designed instruments; unfortunately, as the George Sand story illustrates all too clearly, much has yet to be done to accomplish this task.

What stimulates Lubetzky's work also inspires my own: a recognition of the potential of library catalogs to be effective and intelligible instruments that help users discover valuable resources that they may not have known about before, and which show the relationships present among the items held in the library clearly and unambiguously. I am grateful for Lubetzky's invaluable contribution to the literature and theory of cataloging. It sparked my interest in a topic that has become the center of my professional life, and it remains a source of inspiration and guidance. I am proud to follow in the footsteps of the most important cataloging scholar of this century.

NOTES

1. Seymour Lubetzky, *Principles of Cataloging, Final Report, Phase I: Descriptive Cataloging* (Los Angeles: Institute of Library Research, University of California, 1969), p. 3.

2. Seymour Lubetzky, *Code of Cataloging Rules: Author and Title Entry: An Unfinished Draft for a New Edition of Cataloging Rules, Prepared for the Catalog Code Revision Committee,* with an explanatory commentary by Paul Dunkin (Chicago: American Library Association, 1960), p. ix.

3. Allyson Carlyle, "The Second Objective of the Catalog: An Evaluation of Collocation in Online Catalog Displays" (Ph.D. diss., University of California, Los Angeles, 1994), published in summary form in Allyson Carlyle, "Ordering Author and Work Records: An Evaluation of Collocation in Online Catalog Displays," *Journal of the American Society for Information Science* 47, no. 7 (July 1996): 538–54.

4. Allyson Carlyle, "Fulfilling the Second Objective in the Online Catalog: Schemes for Organizing Author and Work Records into Usable Displays," *Library Resources & Technical Services* 41, no. 2 (1997): 79–100; cf. Barbara B. Tillett, "A Taxonomy of Bibliographic Relationships," *Library Resources & Technical Services* 35, no. 2 (1991): 150–58.

5. Allyson Carlyle, "The Role of Classification in the Creation of Author and Work Displays in Online Catalogues," in *Knowledge Organization for Information Retrieval: Proceedings of the Sixth International Study Conference on Classification Research, Held at University College London 16–18 June 1997* (The Hague: International Federation for Information and Documentation, 1997), p. 90–96.

6. Allyson Carlyle, "User Categorisation of Works: Toward Improved Organisation of Online Catalogue Displays," *Journal of Documentation 55,* no. 2 (March 1999): 184–208.

7. Tillett, "Taxonomy."

8. Ibid.

9. Richard Smiraglia, "Authority Control and the Extent of Derivative Bibliographic Relationships" (Ph.D. diss., University of Chicago, 1992).

6

Main and Added Entries

MICHAEL CARPENTER

My topic is the past and future of main and added entries. I roughly define main entry as the name of the author on the top line of a catalog card or online display, plus the title of the work, plus enough information to identify the edition.[1] Added entries, on the other hand, are the names of additional authors or the title of a book or other object; generally, these other names are used to find the catalog entry for an item.

Historically, catalogs have been available in three forms: the book-form catalog in which the catalog is presented on the pages of a book; the card catalog in which the catalog is presented on separate cards, one per main or added entry; and, finally, the online catalog.

In the book catalog, the main entry has the fullest details to be found about the item cataloged; while a collection of references may provide alternative approaches to the main entry, these references have fewer pieces of information about the item.

In a card catalog, entries take one of two forms: (1) In those catalogs using printed cards, the information about the item cataloged is to be found in every entry in the catalog for the item. This is called unit card technology, because the printed part of the card with its main entry heading is the unit that is repeated for all entries in the catalog. (2)

There may be a single main entry in a typed or handwritten card catalog, plus a collection of either shortened added entries or references to
the main entry. In both the book and the card catalog, the references or
added entries are alternative approaches to a catalog entry for a given
bibliographic item; they should not be confused with references from
varying forms of names of persons, bodies, or titles of works.

In online catalogs, numerous display formats are available. Common
to a large number of online catalog displays is a screen twenty-five lines
down and eighty columns across. The effect of this display is to ensure
that only one full catalog entry can be displayed at a time; such occurs in
many World Wide Web–based catalogs. Furthermore, in the usual screen,
no varying character sizes are available, just regular and boldface.

Similarly, in card catalogs using Online Computer Library Center
(OCLC)–printed cards, most of the entries are printed with a monospaced,
single-font print chain. The displays in both online catalogs and currently
produced catalog cards are thus typographically undistinguished.

The Objectives of the Catalog

The vast majority of cataloging codes in the world today claim to be
based on the "Statement of Principles" issued by the International Conference on Cataloguing Principles held in Paris in 1961. Drawn from various wordings found in Lubetzky's writings of the 1950s,[2] the "Statement
of Principles" (section 2, *Functions of the Catalogue*) states that:

> The catalogue should be an efficient instrument for ascertaining
>
> 2.1 whether the library contains a particular book specified by
>   (a) its author and title, *or*
>   (b) if the author is not named in the book, its title alone, *or*
>   (c) if author and title are inappropriate or insufficient for
>   identification, a suitable substitute for the title; and
>
> 2.2 (a) which works by a particular author and
>   (b) which editions of a particular work are in the library.[3]

Can the catalogs we have today fulfill both of these functions? It
seems clear enough that although a catalog that only displays one item
at a time will achieve the first objective, it will not "be an efficient instrument" for achieving the *second* objective. The second objective requires a

display that shows at least a substantial amount of the range of an author's œuvre, or a number of the available editions. People cannot easily perceive the range of available items one item-screen or one card at a time; as Cutter states, "A card presents to the eye only one title at a time, whereas a printed catalogue generally has all of the author's works on a single page."[4] To be sure, most online catalogs provide for a single- or double-line display of catalog records, but given the monotony of fonts available in the average online catalog screen, plus the repetitious nature of the beginning of the brief entries, the arrangement is far from clear.

A reengineering of online catalog displays is in order. A reengineered screen would display many characters per line, just as in a Windows display on a seventeen-inch or larger monitor. The beginning of the main entry heading would be bold-faced, with subdivisions of the heading in italics, just like the examples of headings in AACR2. A rather ordinary-appearing typeface would be used in the body of the description and even smaller type in the collation and notes. But above all, the author heading would appear only once for a collection of the works of an author or the various editions of a work. Items after the first would be prefaced by a long dash, much in the fashion of the typography of the British Museum catalog or Cutter's catalog of the Boston Athenaeum.

More than catalog interface revision is required, however, for our newly reengineered catalog. Rules would need to be changed. Cataloging rules have two aspects in their logic, aspects not clearly distinguished in any current code. The first aspect is the standard for the record structure: what type of information needs to be gathered? The second aspect is a display standard: what is a useful arrangement of the catalog? Cutter made the distinction by concentrating to a certain extent on display in his section on arrangement. Concentration on the aspect of a code as a display standard would not only give direction to the reengineering effort but also provide guidance in determining what should go into the record structure.

A useful display for the record of a single item is arrangement by author followed by work name (usually the title) and then by enough information to distinguish among editions in a number of useful fashions; that usually is the way we cite items in bibliographies. In Western society, we have generally used authors as a means of identifying works since at least the time of Sumer. Doing so certainly distinguishes works published with identical titles. And authorship clearly forms the basis of the Paris Statement's "functions of the catalogue"; other approaches are either *faute de mieux* or useful supplements.

When people cannot remember the author of a work, or are faced with works of multiple authorship while not remembering the primary author, or are simply looking for materials by subject, provisions exist for added entries based on the names of people or bodies standing in an authorial relationship to the item, by title, or by subject; in addition, numerous types of keyword searching exist. The display in response to the query should still provide author, work, and edition.

In the end, there are no excuses other than financial lassitude and programmer laziness for a user having to specify whether he or she wants an author, title, or subject heading in a catalog query. The user should be able to type in the string of characters representing any of these and get something from the catalog. Card catalogs filed in the dictionary arrangement work that way. Today's catalogs, however, are generally divided by author, title, and subject, making it difficult to find editions of a literary work together with criticism on that work. On the other hand, Cutter's dictionary catalog interfiles the author, subject, more or less most of a title, and more or less most of a form catalog into one convenient whole. With their divided structure, today's online catalogs cause us to make meaningless title-added entries, such as those that are the same as subject headings, or those that contain empty words such as "Introduction to [followed by the same words as a subject heading]."

To make our discussion more specific than a discussion of the relation of catalog structure and main entry, we now turn to added entries.

Added Entries

The "Statement of Principles" specifies that

> 6.4 *Added entries* (or in appropriate cases *references*) should also be made under the names of joint-authors, collaborators, etc., and under the titles of works having their main entry under an author's name, when the title is an important alternative means of identification.

What constitutes "an important alternative means of identification"? Historically, what counts has varied. In the original draft of the British Museum rules (the 73 rules of March 1839, a set of rules written by Anthony Panizzi and his coworkers), the only form of title entries to be found is those for anonymous works; when no name of an author, editor, translator, corporate body, title of a work commented on, or initials can be found, Panizzi prescribes entry under the first substantive, or failing that, the first word in the title is "to be selected as the heading."[5] There is no provision for references from titles. By the time the British Museum Trustees finished revising the rules and gave us the text of the 91 rules in 1841, title entries indeed had disappeared, except as a default means of identifying anonymously published materials, and even the remaining title entries were to be reformulated according to a complex set of rules. Again, there was to be no reference from a title to a main entry.[6] Cutter refers to a "series of London book lists ending in the 'Classified index to the London catalogue of books published in 1816–'51' [in which] references are arranged in the alphabetic order of the words of the title which expressed, or were intended to express, the specific subject of the book."[7] Andrea Crestadoro, assistant to Sampson Low, the publisher of the previously mentioned index, anonymously published a proposal to generate an index to a register of book descriptions.[8] Following through on this idea, Nathaniel B. Shurtleff, one of the founding staff members of the Boston Public Library, started a catalog of books using one main card having all the tracings on it, plus a group of references to that main card.[9] When he became Superintendent of the Boston Public Library, Charles C. Jewett continued the same system and published several versions of the *Index* (really only a listing of references) to that manuscript card catalog. Typical references included subject headings and title entries, inverted where necessary. The title entries often had no reference to the author of the book they were referencing.[10] Cutter quotes Poole in 1854 stating that the catalog of the Boston Mercantile Library had "works of fiction . . . placed under their titles as well as authors."[11]

With respect to title entries, Cutter notes that age of the book, language, size, etc., "are of no importance in a title-entry, the object of which is simply to enable a man to find a book he already knows of, not to select one of many."[12] At the same time, Cutter, in the first edition of his rules, limits title-added entry (reference) to plays, lengthy poems, any other good reason, "works which are entered under the names of societies or governments [on the grounds that many German catalogs fail to recognize such bodies for the purpose of entry]" plus a number of catchword title references. All these references are to the author entries.[13] By the second edition of 1889, Cutter enlarges the list to titles for works in which the "subject-word is not the same as the name of the subject selected by the cataloger"[14] and occasional subtitles and half titles.[15] In his fourth edition, Cutter sums up the requirements for title-added entry thus: "make a title-reference when the author's name is common, the title memorable, or the subject obscure."[16] Because of the growing importance of Library of Congress printed cards, Cutter's fourth edition did not greatly affect cataloging practice in the United States. Instead, when the Library of Congress began to print catalog cards, it started with the third edition of Cutter,[17] together with various memoranda, the revised contents of which became supplementary rules on cards. Card rule 18, "Added Entries (Title)" (printed December 26, 1905), calls for title-added entries for dramas and works of fiction, "practically all entries under headings not taken directly from the title," works with significant or memorable titles, and materials entered under corporate body.[18]

The 1908 code provides for the same cases as those in Cutter and "in all cases where an added entry will insure the ready finding of the book," surely a phrase begging for interpretation.[19]

The LC card rules stayed in force through the early 1940s. Their lack of evident rationale provided the subject matter for Lubetzky's "Titles: Fifth Column of the Catalog," in which Lubetzky analyzes the functions title-added entries should have in the catalog and suggests a substantial reduction in their number: title-added entries that are identical with subject headings or references to them, and convoluted catchword title-added entries, are to be avoided.[20] It must be emphasized that Lubetzky's analysis works in the context of a dictionary catalog, not in that of most divided catalogs. The 1941 draft code has a permissive attitude about added entries, suggesting that individual libraries may vary somewhat; however, it does state a preference for subject headings. Even so, it provides for substantial use of title catchword entries.[21]

One would think that by the time the 1949 code appeared, some of Lubetzky's 1941 advice would have made a difference. Except for minor changes in wording, however, the 1949 provisions are identical to those of the 1941 code.[22]

By the time of the 1967 *Anglo-American Cataloging Rules*, there is only a small list of exceptions to the requirement for title-added entry.[23] In AACR2, the list of exceptions diminishes even more.[24] What happened? I suggest that since the three-way division of catalogs (author, title, subject), which started becoming popular in the mid-1960s, the meaningfulness of restrictions on the use of title-added entries lost their force.[25] The vision of a dictionary catalog had melted away when subject entries were removed from the catalog, not along the lines Lubetzky was finally willing to accept (name entries in one file and topical, nonname, subject headings in the other file),[26] but instead on a mechanical arrangement, resembling the online catalogs of today. Even after the excuse for catalog division has passed, namely the increasing size and complexity of card catalogs, every online catalog I've seen is still divided.

A second thing happened, too. Cataloging description became divorced from headings, or entry, to the point that AACR2 is designed so that one is supposed to derive a description independently of providing access points. At the beginning of the section on the arrangement of headings in all four editions of his rules, Cutter remarks, "This order [of arranging] is easy to remember because it follows the course of cataloguing; *we put down first the author, then the title,* and lastly look inside for the subject" (my emphasis).[27] At times today, when an added entry for a corporate body is needed, and its only justification is through an authorial affiliation on the title page or other chief source of information, the cataloger transcribes the affiliation in the statement of responsibility, often enclosing it in square brackets. Thus, catalogers don't really act as if they believed that description is independent of entry.

In a memorandum he wrote in October of 1943, Lubetzky questions the reasoning behind slavish transcription of the title page when it doesn't serve the purposes of the catalog. Lubetzky asks why we should repeat the name of the author, already provided in the main entry, in the author statement.[28] One could suggest that Panizzi and Cutter surely didn't repeat author statements that were already included in the main entry. They saw the catalog entry as an integrated whole.

A second reason for the shape of catalogs today might be called the access-point mentality, consisting of tacking main and added entries onto a bibliographic description. This mentality goes back to two historical events. Both at the time seemed unavoidable. The first is that Lubetzky's assignments in revising codes came in two parts, the first involving bibliographic description, with entry under consideration only later. Although there is some evidence of integration of author statements and main entries in the 1949 descriptive cataloging rules,[29] the fact that it was separately published from the rules for entry and heading in that year[30] allowed some writers to divorce the two. The second event resulted from the desire to reuse descriptions developed from national bibliographies in library catalogs. The International Standard Bibliographic Descriptions (ISBDs) started life as a common-denominator approach to entries in national bibliographies.[31] Because the United States cannot have a national bibliography (the First Amendment prevents legal deposit legislation, the basis of a national bibliography), we were unlikely to have developed such a standard here. Notice that the objectives for descriptions in national bibliographies are not the same as for library catalogs. One is for legal identification of a particular book, and, by extension, all other copies of that book (a particular issue or edition, but not a work); the other is to tell the library's public what the library has, organized primarily by authors and secondarily by subject matter. What we have with self-standing bibliographic descriptions plus "access points" is essentially a register with an index. The superiority of the so-called index we have in today's online catalogs over those of Crestadoro and Shurtleff in the nineteenth century is that we get to see the description as a blob of text in a one-step operation, rather than having to look it up at a particular place in the printed register.

The register-index catalog is not one that lends itself to arrangement of the entries in a way that readily fulfills the second function of the catalog. It does, however, admirably fulfill the first objective. On the other hand, by allowing one to obtain a single catalog entry on the basis of title alone, it does not readily show the user the full panoply of the library's resources, such as the editions it holds of a work with their varying titles, nor does it send the reader to the rest of the author's works.

What should the catalog of tomorrow look like? How should it operate? Clearly, if a user looks up a particular author, all that author's works will appear in a usable arrangement. If a title is sought, and only one author has composed something with that title, entries for all the editions will appear. If more than one author has composed something with the sought title, the user will be asked to choose the one he or she wants. After the full display, the call number or information as to how you can get the item will appear; the catalog may even take the user to the desired website. But he or she will first see the editions of the work and the other works of the author that the library has. If a subject is sought, editions of each work with that subject heading will appear, arranged by author, work, and edition. If the user wants more works by a particular author, all he or she has to do is point to the author's name, and the full panoply of that author's œuvre will appear. We will then be working with a catalog that, as a minimum, is faithful to the Paris Principles.

NOTES

1. Other definitions are current, too. For an analysis, see Michael Carpenter, "Main Entry," in *The Conceptual Foundations of Descriptive Cataloging*, ed. Elaine Svenonius (San Diego: Academic Press, 1989), p. 73–95.

2. See, among others, Seymour Lubetzky, *Cataloging Rules and Principles: A Critique of the A.L.A. Rules for Entry and a Proposed Design for Their Revision* (Washington, D.C.: Library of Congress, 1953; reprint, High Wycombe, England : Published for the College of Librarianship, Wales, by University Microfilms, 1970), p. 36; "Code for Cataloging: Authors and Titles," rev. ed., partial draft (n.p., 1956 [i.e., 1958]), p. 3; *Code of Cataloging Rules: Bibliographic Entry and Description: A Partial and Tentative Draft for a New Edition of Bibliographic Cataloging Rules, Prepared for the Catalog Code Revision Committee* ([Chicago]: American Library Association, Resources and Technical Services Division, Cataloging and Classification Section, Catalog Code Revision Committee, 1958), p. 2; *Code of Cataloging Rules: Author and Title Entry: An Unfinished Draft for a New Edition of Cataloging Rules, Prepared for the Catalog Code Revision Committee*, with an explanatory commentary by Paul Dunkin (Chicago: American Library Association, 1960), p. ix–x; *Code of Cataloging Rules: Author and Title Entry. Additions, Revisions and Changes Prepared in Light of Discussions of the March 1960 Draft for Consideration of the Catalog Code Revision Committee* (Chicago: American Library Association, 1961), p. 2.

3. International Conference on Cataloguing Principles, *Statement of Principles Adopted at the International Conference on Cataloguing Principles, Paris, October 1961*, annotated ed. with commentary and examples, ed. Eva Verona (London: British Museum; International Federation of Library Associations (Committee on Cataloguing), 1971), p. xiii.

4. Charles A. Cutter, "Library Catalogues," in United States, Bureau of Education, *Public Libraries in the United States of America: Their History, Condition, and Management: Special Report, Part I* (Washington, D.C.: Government Printing Office, 1876; reprint, Urbana: University of Illinois, Graduate School of Library Science, 1966?), p. 535.

5. British Museum, *Alphabetical Catalogue of Printed Books: Rules to Be Observed in Preparing and Entering Titles* (London: [British Museum, March 1839]).

6. Anthony Panizzi, "Rules for the Compilation of the Catalogue," in British Museum, Dept. of Printed Books, *Catalogue of Printed Books in the British Museum* (London: Printed by Order of the Trustees, 1841), vol. 1, p. v–ix, reprinted in *Foundations of Cataloging: A Sourcebook*, ed. Michael Carpenter and Elaine Svenonius (Littleton, Colo.: Libraries Unlimited, 1985), p. 3–14.

7. Cutter, "Library Catalogues," p. 534–35.

8. Andrea Crestadoro, *The Art of Making Catalogues of Libraries, or, A Method to Obtain in a Short Time a Most Perfect, Complete, and Satisfactory Printed Catalogue of the British Museum Library, by a Reader Therein* (London: Published and sold by The Literary, Scientific & Artistic Reference Office, 1856).

9. Nathaniel B. Shurtleff, *A Decimal System for the Arrangement and Administration of Libraries* (Boston: Privately Printed, 1856).

10. Not only was production of the cards contracted out to the English suppliers of the books that Joshua Bates was sending to the library, but there was no main entry even on the manuscript card.

11. Cutter, "Library Catalogues," p. 534.

12. Ibid., p. 529, note 1.

13. Charles A. Cutter, "Rules for a Printed Dictionary Catalogue," in United States, Bureau of Education, *Public Libraries in the United States of America: Their History, Condition, and Management: Special Report, Part II* (Washington, D.C.: Government Printing Office, 1876), p. 34–36, rules 59–64.

14. Charles A. Cutter, *Rules for a Dictionary Catalogue,* 2nd ed., with corrections and additions (Washington, D.C.: Government Printing Office, 1889), p. 44, rule 88b.

15. Ibid., p. 45, rule 90.

16. Charles A. Cutter, *Rules for a Dictionary Catalogue,* 4th ed., rewritten (Washington, D.C.: Government Printing Office, 1904; reprint, London: Republished by the Library Association, 1962), p. 63.

17. Charles A. Cutter, *Rules for a Dictionary Catalogue,* 3rd ed., with corrections and additions and an alphabetical index (Washington, D.C.: Government Printing Office, 1891).

18. Library of Congress, *Special Rules on Cataloging to Supplement A.L.A.,* advance ed., 1–21 (Washington, D.C.: Government Printing Office, Library Division, 1906), p. 24.

19. *Catalog Rules: Author and Title Entries,* comp. Committees of the American Library Association and the (British) Library Association, American ed. (Chicago: American Library Association, Publishing Board, 1908), p. 56, rule 169.

20. Seymour Lubetzky, "Titles: Fifth Column of the Catalog," *Library Quarterly* 11 (Oct. 1941): 412–30.

21. American Library Association, Catalog Code Revision Committee, *A.L.A. Catalog Rules: Author and Title Entries,* prelim. American 2nd ed. (Chicago: American Library Association, 1941), p. 231–32, rule 223.

22. American Library Association, Division of Cataloging and Classification, *A.L.A. Cataloging Rules for Author and Title Entries,* 2nd ed., ed. Clara Beetle (Chicago: American Library Association, 1949), p. 220–21, rule 157.

23. *Anglo-American Cataloging Rules. North American Text* (Chicago: American Library Association, 1967), p. 70–72, rule 33.

24. *Anglo-American Cataloguing Rules,* 2nd ed., 1998 revision (Ottawa: Canadian Library Association; Chicago: American Library Association, 1998), p. 356–57, rule 21.30J.

25. Lubetzky ("Crisis in the Catalog," *Catalogers' and Classifiers' Yearbook* 8 (1940): 48–54) describes the issues in dividing catalogs, and later suggests that a modified vertical division is the best of the alternatives to a single catalog (*Principles of Cataloging: Final Report, Phase I: Descriptive Cataloging* (Los Angeles: University of California Institute of Library Research, 1969), p. 74–75). The most substantial discussion of a catalog divided among authors, titles, and subjects is found in Joseph Z. Nitecki, "The Title Catalog: A Third Dimension," *College and Research Libraries* 29 (September 1968): 431–36.

26. Lubetzky, *Principles of Cataloging,* p. 79.

27. Cutter, "Rules for a Printed Dictionary Catalogue" (1876), p. 68, rule 170; *Rules for a Dictionary Catalog,* 2nd ed. (Washington, D.C.: Government Printing Office, 1889), p. 83, rule 214; 3rd ed. (1891), p. 83, rule 214; 4th ed. (1904), p. 111, rule 300.

28. Seymour Lubetzky, "Analysis of the Principal Weaknesses of Current Descriptive Cataloging and Suggested Principles to Guide Its Rules and Practice," prepared as a basis for discussion in conferences to be held by the Director of the Processing Department and Chief of the Descriptive Cataloging Division, Library of Congress, with library administrators and catalogers (October 1943, hectographed), p. 2–3.

29. Library of Congress, Descriptive Cataloging Division, *Rules for Descriptive Cataloging in the Library of Congress (Adopted by the American Library Association)* (Washington, D.C.: Library of Congress, 1949).

30. *A.L.A. Cataloging Rules for Author and Title Entries.*

31. Evidence for these assertions can be found in the prefatory material relating to aims of the description in early documents for what became the ISBD, for example: Michael Gorman, "Bibliographical Data in National Bibliography Entries: A Report on Descriptive Cataloging Made for UNESCO and IFLA," final revised version (1968), p. 5 (typescript reproduction in American Library Association archives, University of Illinois, Urbana-Champaign); and Michael Gorman, "Standard Bibliographic Description (For Single and Multivolume Monographs): A Comprehensive and International Standard for the Recording of Bibliographic Data, Prepared for the I.M.C.E. Working Party on the Standard Bibliographic Description," July 1970, p. 2 (multilithed original in Library of Congress Manuscript Division).

7

Lubetzky's Work Principle

MARTHA M. YEE

Lubetzky is an immigrant who came to America bearing gifts. One of the most important was the concept that "book" and "work" are coextensive only in the case of a work that has been published only once, and therefore exists in only one edition. While it is possible that the majority of works collected by large research libraries fall into the category of works existing in only one edition, these are probably not the works most sought and used. If these were works of use to many different people over a long period of time, they would probably exist in multiple editions. As soon as a work goes into multiple editions, multiple title pages representing that work exist, title pages that can carry variants in the title of the work, variants in the author or authors' names, different subtitles, different series, different subsidiary authors, such as translators, editors, etc. Lubetzky the immigrant chose a very American example to illustrate this point: Ralph Waldo Emerson's famous essay suggesting that America's days of dependence on European scholarship were over, "The American Scholar"; the earliest editions of this essay were published as "An Oration Delivered before the Phi Beta Kappa Society, at Cambridge, August 31, 1837."[1] Once these kinds of variations begin to occur, human intervention is required to ensure that a user seeking a work is allowed to choose among all editions of that work held by the library.

The search for a known work is probably the most common type of search conducted in large research libraries. User studies are very difficult to interpret in this regard, because of the propensity for users to do subject searches or include subject terms in their searches when looking for a known work, and because of the tendency of online public access catalogs (OPACs) to force users to search under *either* author *or* title; probably most author searches should be counted as known-work searches for this reason. Contrary to some reports, the Council on Library Resources (CLR) catalog use studies did not demonstrate conclusively that subject searching predominates over other kinds of searching; "author-subject," "title-subject," and "author-title-subject" searches were counted as subject searches, although it seems probable that many such searches were known-work searches done by users who knew the subject of the work sought.[2] Because known-work searching is so commonly done, Lubetzky's contribution to the improvement of service to users of catalogs in this country was immense.

Like all great principles, Lubetzky's principles of cataloging sound simple and self-evident. Also like all great principles, they are not so easy to apply in all cases. At times, it is not so easy to decide whether two items represent two different editions of the same work, or whether they represent two different works that are related to each other. At times, it is not easy to decide on the best way to *name* a work, to facilitate its collocation: when is it best to name a work using both its author and title, and when is it preferable to name a work using its title alone? Or if the work is known in many languages, which language should be preferred? And, finally, for Lubetzky's principles to benefit catalog users everywhere, they must be put into practice in an elaborate system of shared cataloging that has grown up in this country in an extremely federated and decentralized manner. This shared system now consists of multiple national databases and multiple local online catalogs, each with its own nonstandard system design, with bibliographic records and authority records flying back and forth among them, but no single catalog to catalog against, when trying to determine if the name of a work is unique, or if it needs authority work to break conflicts with other works with the same name. Partly because of a lack of resources and partly because of the lack of a single catalog against which to catalog, many libraries have declined to follow Lubetzky's good advice and still refuse to use uniform titles to collocate the editions of a work. Thus, editions of Emerson's "American Scholar" are still not collocated in ORION, UCLA's online catalog.

The Same Work? Or Two Different Works?

In the following discussion, current practice regarding cases when two items are represented as the same work and when they are different works is deduced from the *Anglo-American Cataloguing Rules,* 2nd ed., 1998 revision (AACR2R) based on main-entry practice. Main entry is an alphabet-dependent device for carrying out the second cataloging objective, i.e., for displaying together all the works of an author and all the editions of a work. Among other things, the main entry is the standard citation form for a work. When two items are given the same main entry, they are represented as being the same work. When two items are given different main entries, they are represented as being different works. Main entry consists of the author (if there is one) and the title (uniform title if there is one, title on item otherwise).

Sometimes Lubetzky's principles are so simple to apply, we do it without thinking about it. If two items represent themselves as being the same work, for example, our practice has always been to consider them the same work if the only differences between them consist of one or more of the following:

- different publisher,
- different publication date,
- different physical format,
- different edition statement but same text (e.g., "microform edition").

In fact, many of us would argue that if those are the *only* changes, the two items even represent the same *edition* of the same work, and can be described on a single bibliographic record. This is the multiple-versions issue. Be that as it may, the work decision is simple and straightforward: same work, i.e., same main entry.

If two items represent themselves as the same work, and the only differences between them consist of one or more of the following:

- different title;
- different series;
- different statement of responsibility, such as variation in the author's name or changes in subsidiary authorship such as inclusion of a different translator or editor;
- different edition statement (connected to change in text, e.g., different extent);
- resetting of type (usually signaled by different paging);
- in nonbook materials, other changes in actual extent, such as playing time;
- difference in presence or absence of illustrations in physical description,

current practice is to consider the two items to be two editions of the same work, i.e., separate bibliographic records, each with the same main entry. Again, this decision is usually simple and straightforward.

Some decisions are not so simple. The following decisions about changes that create a new edition of a work and changes that create a new work have been recorded in AACR2R and constitute current practice. (Neither Lubetzky nor I agree with all of current practice, by the way.) Under current practice, we consider the following changes not to be substantial enough to cause the creation of a new work (signaled by the retention of the same main entry as the original work):

- translation into another language;
- addition of illustrations to a text;
- revision of a text by the same author(s) as the original;
- addition of commentary or biographical/critical material when the original work is emphasized in title-page representation;
- reproduction of an artwork;
- arrangement, transcription, etc., of the work of a composer;
- providing a choreography for an existing musical work, such as a ballet;
- adding an instrumental accompaniment or additional parts to a musical work;
- performing a musical work on a sound recording.

We consider the following changes substantial enough to cause the creation of a new work (signaled by a change in main entry):

- rewriting of a text in another form, e.g., the dramatization of a novel;
- filming of a play;
- adaptation of an artwork from one medium to another (e.g., an engraving of a painting);
- changing of the title of a work entered under title (including both monographs and serials);
- revision of a text accompanied by a change in representation of authorship or change in title;
- addition of commentary or biographical/critical material when the commentary or biographical/critical material is emphasized in title-page representation;
- free transcription of the work of a composer;
- merely basing a musical work on other music, e.g., variations on a theme;
- setting a preexisting text to music.

Some of these decisions were not so easy to make and are a cause of continuing controversy. Much of the controversy may stem from the fact that we have not yet completely come to terms with the phenomenon of mixed responsibility. According to the AACR2R glossary, a work of mixed responsibility is one in which different persons or bodies contribute to its intellectual or artistic content by performing different kinds of activities (e.g., adapting or illustrating a work written by another person). Mixed responsibility is very common in my field (film and television). I see signs that it is likely to be very common in the production of original works for distribution by way of the Web, and it is even possible that it represents a general trend in the creation of works of art, literature, and music. Films are classic cases of mixed responsibility. Major contributions to a film work are made by the writer, the director, the cinematographer, and the editor, and these are often four different people. Film scholars are passionately interested in studying the work of all four, but they tend to identify and cite works by title, rather than selecting one function as predominant over the others, and citing works by, for example, director or writer.

The following problematic categories of works will be briefly discussed: works of photography, works intended for performance (including music, drama, and dance), texts with illustrations, music with words, works produced in stages, revised editions, spatial data, and serials (electronic and otherwise).

Works of Photography

Photography is peculiar. It can: (1) merely record or represent a previously existing work, and serve as a surrogate for it or an embodiment of it; (2) it can be a creative work in its own right, or (3) it can be *both* surrogate/embodiment *and* work in its own right. Ultimately, a judgment must be made whether it is a creative work in its own right, and librarians, who bend over backwards to be objective and nonjudgmental, are reluctant to make such judgments.

Image catalogers need to make a clear decision about what is being described to prevent the creation of a confusing record; the work that is not described must be treated as a related work of some type. AACR2R does not yet provide much guidance for decisions of this kind, although it does call for entering a reproduction, such as a slide of a work of art, under the heading for the original work (21.16B). Because slide collections are created and used as surrogates for art originals, which may be located at remote sites that are expensive or impossible to visit, a reproduction of an art original is treated as if it were the art original itself. This is true even though the slide reproduction is almost always different in scale and different in medium (for any art original other than a photograph).

When a work is represented in another work that *is* of interest, such as a photographic work or the work of another artist, a decision must be made. Michael Kenna's photographs of Le Notre's gardens, recently shown at the Huntington Library, for example, should probably be considered primarily the work of Michael Kenna, but related to the work of Le Notre.[3] The current popularity of performance art is raising similar problems. When the work of a performance artist is documented by another artist, the latter a photographer or cinematographer, the problems are similar. Also, the proliferation of images of Mona Lisa in fine art, on T-shirts, in Wegman photos, reflected on magazine covers, on an apron, over and over by Warhol, etc., forces us to realize that reproduction of an image cannot always be held to be simply a copy (manifestation) of the original.[4]

Film is a relatively new medium of expression (only 100 years old) that is fundamentally a work of photography, in which meaning is expressed by means of the visual composition of frames, cutting, camera angles, and rhythm and timing of the action before the camera. While film draws on all previous art forms (painting, writing, sculpture, architecture, music, dance), it is fundamentally a new art form. As such, adaptation is necessary to turn any previously existing work into a work in this form.

The problem is, of course, that just as all text is not belles lettres, not all films are films, i.e., cinematic works, such as those previously described. Film can also be used as a "mere recording medium," as in the case of scientific record film, anthropological film, and so forth. In truth, film can be put to as many varied uses as text can.

How can catalogers tell whether they are dealing with a cinematic work or instead with film as a "mere recording medium"? One clue lies in the functions credited on the film: if a cinematographer, an editor, a screenwriter, and a director are involved, it is highly likely that the work is a cinematic work, as these are the kinds of functions that result in the expression of meaning using visual composition of frames, cutting, camera angles, and rhythm and timing of the action before the camera.

Works Intended for Performance

Music

In the music field, the dominant mode of production for hundreds of years has been composition by a single composer. A piece of written or printed music usually has a single composer. It often has a nondistinctive title and is best known by the name of its composer.

Music, however, is written in the anticipation of its performance. For centuries, we have been able to collect only the written music, not the performances. With the advent of recording mechanisms in the latter part of the nineteenth century, it became possible to begin to collect many different performances of the same musical work. Technically, all performances are works of mixed responsibility, for both composer and performer are responsible for a performed work. In practice, however, music scholars have considered the work of the performer a subsidiary type of authorship, similar to that of a translator of a text. Performer and translator both are seen as conduits that allow the work to pass from its creator to its audience, with faithfulness to the original work being one of the hallmarks of an effective and praiseworthy conduit.

To someone like myself who is not an expert music cataloger, it seems that it would be helpful to use a more principled approach toward when improvisation, arrangement, or other similar change to a musical work is extensive enough to justify considering it a new work (i.e., a type of adaptation). What is essential about a musical work that persists through improvisation, arrangement, etc.? Is it melody? Are there musical forms analogous to "play" and "novel" such that movement from one form to the other constitutes adaptation? (See also a following section specifically on improvisation.)

Dramatico-Musical Works

As with music, for centuries the only things libraries could collect were the texts and printed music of works intended for performance, such as plays or operas. The performances themselves could not be recorded and thus could not be collected. There is a possibility that dramatico-musical works, however, when seen as works intended for performance, rather than as textual or musical works, are essentially works of mixed responsibility that cannot exist as performed works without the participation of many different people performing many different functions.

Actually, three layers of creative activity are going on in the creation of a dramatico-musical work that is then filmed: (1) There is composition of the original text or music (we will ignore the problem of opera librettos for now). (2) There are the decisions that go into actually producing the play or opera in a live performance (lighting, sets, costume design, casting, various voicings of the arias, and so forth). (3) Finally, there are the creative decisions that go into making a cinematic work: camera angles, composition of frames, cutting, etc. It is the third layer that I am convinced constitutes a kind of adaptation, such that the play or opera becomes a film, a different work—a photographic work, not a musical work (but one related to the opera on which it is based). I am willing to concede that when film is used as a mere recording medium, it is not a cinematic work. If a screenwriter, an editor, and a cinematographer are credited, however, I recommend that it be considered a new cinematic work. If this approach were to be taken, it would be crucial to make an added entry for the main entry of any preexisting work that is adapted into a new work in the course of performance.

A more logical (but very radical) approach should be examined at least. If it is desired to consider *all* performances of a particular dramatico-musical work as the same work, no matter what the medium, we could consider all dramatico-musical works to be inherently works of mixed responsibility, unable to exist without the work of many different people carrying out many different functions, and therefore entered under title. Thus, all librettos, scores, performances, and films of *Magic Flute* would be entered under title. We would then doubtless be committing ourselves to elaborate uniform titles to allow versions of versions to be linked up to each other. For example, the various versions of Ingmar Bergman's *Magic Flute* would need to be subcollocated along with its sound track, its scripts, works about it, videodisc versions with additional material, etc. It is interesting to note in this connection that dramatico-musical works tend to have fairly distinctive titles compared to some other types of musical works (e.g., *Don Giovanni* or *Hamlet* versus the Fifth Symphony), and their performances can easily be advertised without using the names of composers or playwrights.

The fundamental question, though, might be: can Mozart or Shakespeare really be the authors of works of photography, given that photography did not exist in their time?

Musical Performances Involving Improvisation

Is there adequate consensus yet about whether jazz improvisation creates editions of previously existing works or whether, on the contrary, it constitutes a kind of composition on the fly, thereby creating new works? For example, the song "All of Me" was written by Gerald Marks (music) and Seymour Simons (lyrics). It has been performed by the following jazz artists: Billie Holiday, Erroll Garner, Frank Sinatra, Sidney Bechet, and Louis Armstrong, among others. If an analytical entry is being made for Erroll Garner's performance, should this be treated as an edition of the song, the music for which was composed by Gerald Marks (Marks, Gerald. All of me)? Or should it be treated as a new related work composed by Erroll Garner in the course of his jazz performance (Garner, Erroll. All of me)? Or is "All of Me" itself fundamentally a work of mixed responsibility (lyrics, music, and performance) that is most appropriately identified and cited by title? These queries involve both the question of what is a musical work and how a musical work should be identified when it is a work of mixed responsibility (i.e., should it be identified by using one predominant author and the title for the main entry, or using the title alone for the main entry)?

Dance

The dance field has come to see performances of dance works as works of mixed responsibility to be entered under title, although this is not yet reflected in AACR2.

Texts with Illustrations

Traditionally, texts with illustrations have been entered under the author of the text. It is possible that in fields such as children's literature, however, this is somewhat artificial. As more and more visual and audio segments are added to electronic versions of previously existing texts, it may become harder and harder to argue for the predominance of text. Librarians have a definite bias toward text and music over visual content, perhaps because visual content is associated in our minds with preliterate cultures and we are passionate advocates of literacy, and perhaps because historically our collections have been primarily textual. We must be careful, however, not to slight all of the parts of our cultural heritage that are visual in nature, and we must be careful not to ignore the needs of users of materials held in our collections that are wholly or partially visual.

Music with Words

Currently, music catalogers consider musical works that include words (such as librettos or lyrics) to be primarily musical, rather than works of mixed responsibility. When the words change, but the music stays the same, music catalogers consider it still the same work. I recently had occasion to catalog a newsreel story about the famous Marian Anderson concert in 1939 in front of the Lincoln Memorial. The newsreel includes her complete performance of "America" ("from every mountainside, let freedom ring"). I wanted to make an added entry for the song and was disconcerted to discover that the main entry for it is "God Save the King," because it uses the melody of the latter. In other words, the change in the lyrics to the song was not considered significant enough to create a new related work. The music catalogers, however, lost their nerve when it came to entering the "Star-Spangled Banner" under "To Anacreon in Heaven"!

Neil Hughes, a music cataloger who has been discussing these issues with me, points out that "to musicians, the words are part of the music, because vowel sounds, sibilants, frontal plosives, etc.—even when part of a meaning-laden text in a modern language and not just vocalizing—are all pure musical elements because they are sound and because they are considered as such by the composer when choosing a text to set, and when creating the instrumental accompaniment, note by note." But surely this is true only for music specialists, and even for them, only some of the time; many users of music respond to the words as much as to the music. Marian Anderson, for one, probably chose the song she sang more for the words than for the sibilants. Is the song Marian Anderson sang really "God Save the King"?

Works Produced in Stages

Creating a work of mixed responsibility, such as a film, is a complex effort. Many pieces must be prepared ahead of time, such as the various drafts of the screenplay, the costume designs, the musical scores, etc. Some can be separately published, such as the sound track and the screenplay. Current practice is to treat each of these pieces as a separate work, each to be entered under its own "author." I wonder whether it might be helpful to users of these materials to consider the creations that result during the course of the preparation of a final work, such as a film, as a part of that final work, to be identified primarily by (i.e., entered under) a uniform title that begins with the title of the film.

Revised Editions

Currently, AACR2R Rules 21.6C1 and 21.12 call for treating revised editions as new works whenever the representation of authorship changes, including simple transposition of the names of two authors on a title page. Such revisions are also treated as new works whenever the title changes. These practices mean that a user can only be assured of finding the latest edition of a text (or other work subject to revision over time) in a library that has cataloging records for every earlier edition, so that the chain-related work-added entries can gradually lead the user from his or her citation to the latest edition. It seems likely that users consider all of these editions to represent the same work, and that they would find it useful to see the editions in one place, so they could be sure of getting the latest, most current edition, and so scientists and historians could more easily survey the library's holdings of earlier editions of a prominent text or other work subject to extensive revision over time. A definition of work that allowed for change in authorship, editorship, or title of a text without the text becoming a new work could help library users in a number of fields that make heavy use of texts (e.g., law and medicine).

Spatial Data

Spatial data includes maps, aerial photographs, remote sensing images, atlases, and globes. How does the concept of work function in the field of spatial data? Can a flat map be made into a globe and still be the same work? Note that any two-dimensional map is trying to represent a three-dimensional reality, so it is probably artificial to forbid a two-dimensional work from having a three-dimensional version that is the same work. When are two items considered two different versions or editions of the same work (i.e., when are they given the same main entry, despite intellectual or artistic differences between them that require making a separate record to express them)? Map catalogers do seem to recognize the concept of edition. The U.S. Geological Survey's 1939 map of Golden, Colorado, for example, has an edition with revisions shown in purple compiled from aerial photographs taken in 1978. At any rate, these two maps are given the same main entry, which would seem to imply that they are considered the same work. It would be useful to ask some map catalogers who were theoretically inclined to investigate whether or not a preexisting map can be changed to such a degree that it should be considered a new work, related to the preexisting work, and if so, whether one can define the nature of such changes in a principled way.

Serials, Electronic and Otherwise

Following another of Lubetzky's principles, that of successive entry for serials, currently change of title of a serial work leads to the creation of a new main entry in AACR2R; in other words, change of title causes the creation of a new, related work. The various related works that make up the history of a given serial can only be assembled by a user who happens to be in a library that holds issues entered under each title the serial has held. If there are any missing links, the run cannot be assembled. Is this really the right way to conceive of a serial work? Does it really correspond to the way users conceptualize serial works? This may be a rare case in which Lubetzky recommended an approach that was practically sound at the time, but not theoretically sound for the long term.

Now that serials are beginning to be distributed electronically, their nature as works is beginning to change in rather profound ways. A serial distributed as issues in text form can now exist simultaneously in electronic form as a continuously updated database consisting of all of the articles ever published in that serial, extending across title changes. In other words, such a database can easily contain articles from a serial that has changed its title several times. Users surely consider both the database and the journal they seek (under any title it has held) as different versions of the same work.

Interactive Multimedia

When preexisting works are reissued with interactive multimedia commentary, biographical/critical information, and so forth, and are still represented as being the original work, it would be best to consider them editions of the preexisting work, for we do the same for noninteractive multimedia editions of a work published with commentary or biographical/critical material, as long as the original work is emphasized in title-page representation. Also, when an existing print work acquires an online multimedia version (e.g., *Encyclopaedia Britannica* and *Britannica Online*), it would be desirable to treat them as editions of the same work.

Pure Categories of Content

I wonder if it would be helpful to consider whether or not there might be a few pure categories of content, with the hypothesis being that a work in one of the eight categories of content that follow cannot be transformed into a work in another of the eight categories without becoming a new work:

1. text
2. music (defined as a work fundamentally comprised of music, either musical notation (typed, printed, or handwritten) or actual sound, i.e., performed music)
3. still image
4. moving image (defined as a work fundamentally comprised of moving images, which often (but not necessarily) has text and sound integrated to make a single work; includes recorded dance performance as well as dance notation, for dance consists of movement (moving image) plus sound)
5. spatial data
6. three-dimensional objects
7. numeric data
8. computer programs

Of course, this hypothesis would need testing by research. The potential utility of this approach is as follows: if we can delineate the fundamental types of content, it might help in defining the concept of *work*, and it might help us determine when a previously existing work has been modified so much it has become a new work.

Mixed Works

Works that do not fall wholly into the eight categories are mixed. In some cases, one type of content predominates; in others, no type predominates. Works for which one type of content predominates include: texts with illustrations (which can now include musical and audiovisual illustrations) and music with words (opera, lieder, etc.). However, refer to the earlier discussion concerning the advisability of considering music to be predominant. In these cases, judgment will be required to determine primacy. The other category of mixed works is those that are fundamentally mixed with no type of content predominant. Examples include: dance (choreography and music; but, again refer to the early discussion); interactive multimedia and other electronic resources that mix text, sound, and image; and kits.

Once different types of content are combined in a single work, the pure content approach is no longer useful. We must either assign predominance to one of two types of content, or we must decline to assign predominance and treat the work as a work of mixed responsibility identified by title alone (unless, of course, all functions were carried out by one person).

How to Name a Work—the Main Entry

In case anyone does not understand what the main entry does, I will quickly try to point out at least some of its functions. First, as noted previously, main entry is an alphabet-dependent device for carrying out the second cataloging objective, i.e., for displaying together all the works of an author and all the editions of a work. Among other things, the main entry is the standard citation form for a work. In its role, the main entry can be used as a collocation point for editions of that work, works about that work, analytic added entries made when another work contains that work, works related to that work, such as adaptations, or serials with changed titles, or revised editions with changed titles, and so forth. Many of these will collocate *only* at the main entry. When making an analytic, for example, a cataloger must choose one standard citation form for the work, and only if the user searches using that standard citation will he or she learn about the existence of the analytic.

Once a standard citation form for a work has been established, it can also be used to display that work in summary displays of the hundreds of works that may easily be retrieved on many kinds of searches, such as subject searches, genre searches, title keyword searches, etc. A well-designed main entry will allow users to scan quickly through a large retrieval set, accepting or rejecting works based on their authorship characteristics. Without main entries, it would not be possible to allow users the option of a display by author (see Figure 1).

Main-entry displays are particularly useful under subject headings, as the titles of works on a subject frequently begin with the same or similar words to those used in the heading. In contrast, an author display provides more differentiation among the works retrieved, allowing identification of (and either acceptance or rejection of) conference publications, works emanating from corporate bodies, works of single personal

FIGURE 1 Works Given the LC Subject Heading SMOKING in
Main-Entry Order

1. Ashton, Heather. Smoking : psychology and pharmacology. 1982.
2. Brown, Clyde Perry. Cigarette smoking and blood lead levels in occupationally exposed workers. 1982.
3. California. Office of the Attorney General. Smoking by minors; a report on the present state of the law. [1969]
4. Cigarette smoking : a clinical guide to assessment and treatment. c1992.
5. Council for Tobacco Research. Report of the scientific director.
6. Doyle, Nancy. Smoking, a habit that should be broken. 1979.
7. Dunn, William L. Smoking behavior : motives and incentives. 1973.
8. Gottsegen, Jack Jacob, 1907- Tobacco, a study of its consumption in the United States. 1940.
9. Howson, Christopher Paul. Cigarette smoking and the use of health services. 1983.
10. Krogh, David. Smoking : the artificial passion. c1991.
11. Kujala, Pekka. Smoking, respiratory symptoms and ventilatory capacity in young men : with a note on physical fitness and acute respiratory infections. 1981.
12. Levy, Robert A. Tobacco Medicaid litigation : snuffing out the rule of law. [1997]
13. Mausner, Bernard, 1920- Smoking: a behavioral analysis. [1971]
14. National Cancer Institute (U.S.) Smoking, tobacco, and cancer program, 1985 report. 1986.
15. National Cancer Institute (U.S.) Smoking, tobacco, and cancer program, annual report, 1983. [1984]
16. National Cancer Institute (U.S.). Office of Cancer Communications. The smoking digest : progress report on a nation kicking the habit. [1977]
17. National Research Conference on Smoking Behavior (2nd : 1966 : University of Arizona) Studies and issues in smoking behavior. [1967]
18. Neuberger, Maurine B. Smoke screen : tobacco and the public welfare. [1963]
19. Smoking and aging. c1984.
20. Smoking and arterial disease. 1981.
21. Smoking and health : a report of the Surgeon General. [1979]
22. Smoking and health bulletin.
23. Smoking in the workplace : a review of arbitration decisions. 1988.
24. Tobacco smoke and the nonsmoker. 1988.
25. United States. Division of Dental Public Health and Resources. Smoking and oral cancer. [1964]
26. United States. Surgeon General's Advisory Committee on Smoking and Health. Smoking and health; report of the advisory committee to the Surgeon General of the Public Health Service. 1964.

authorship, works by experts in the field (or at least authors who have written on this subject more than once), etc. (see Figure 2). The fact that library catalogs can produce main-entry displays (or alphabetical author listings) is one of the many ways in which they are superior to the Internet (see Figure 3).

Main entry based on authorship is an absolute necessity when it comes to displaying works of prolific authors that have nondistinctive titles—such as most musical works. Contrast the display by author in Figure 4 with the display of the same works by title in Figure 5.

Creating a standard citation form for a work (the main entry) allows the compression of displays of many editions of a particular work, as well as works about it and works related to it, so users can better scan through the large retrieval sets that are giving them so much difficulty in online public access catalogs. Consider, for example, displays that could be offered to a user interested in browsing through the works of Shakespeare, with a specific interest in *Macbeth* (see Figure 6).

It is possible that a change in the MARC 21 format to specifically identify related work-added entries as performance-added entries could lead to online catalog displays that might prevent undue confusion for users who consider a performance (even one adapted into a cinematic work) and a work intended for performance to be the same work. Currently, the second indicator of a MARC 21 7XX added-entry field for a work can be set to 2 when the work is actually contained within the work cataloged. If the same second indicator were given another value for performance, it would potentially allow for the type of display shown in Figure 7 to the user who has chosen line 10 in order to look at the library's editions of *Macbeth*.

Of course, this still dodges the question of which films are mere recordings of a performance (same work) and which are adaptations (new works), and whether this distinction should be made visible to users in displays. The following illustrates what such a distinction could look like, if we decided to make it.

Shakespeare, William, 1564–1616. Macbeth.

1. Editions of Macbeth.
2. Performances of Macbeth.
3. Films based on Macbeth.
4. Other works related to Macbeth.
5. Works about Macbeth.

FIGURE 2   Works Given the LC Subject Heading SMOKING Listed by Title

1. Cigarette smoking : a clinical guide to assessment and treatment. c1992.
2. Cigarette smoking and blood lead levels in occupationally exposed workers. 1982.
3. Cigarette smoking and the use of health services. 1983.
4. Report of the scientific director.
5. Smoke screen : tobacco and the public welfare. [1963]
6. Smoking : a behavioral analysis. [1971]
7. Smoking : psychology and pharmacology. 1982.
8. Smoking : the artificial passion. c1991.
9. Smoking, a habit that should be broken. 1979.
10. Smoking and aging. c1984.
11. Smoking and arterial disease. 1981.
12. Smoking and health : a report of the Surgeon General. [1979]
13. Smoking and health; report of the advisory committee to the Surgeon General of the Public Health Service. 1964.
14. Smoking and health bulletin.
15. Smoking and oral cancer. 1964.
16. Smoking behavior : motives and incentives. 1973.
17. Smoking by minors; a report on the present state of the law. 1969.
18. The smoking digest : progress report on a nation kicking the habit. [1977]
19. Smoking in the workplace : a review of arbitration decisions. 1988.
20. Smoking, respiratory symptoms and ventilatory capacity in young men : with a note on physical fitness and acute respiratory infections. 1981.
21. Smoking, tobacco, and cancer program, 1985 report. 1986.
22. Smoking, tobacco, and cancer program, annual report, 1983. [1984]
23. Studies and issues in smoking behavior. [1967]
24. Tobacco, a study of its consumption in the United States. 1940.
25. Tobacco Medicaid litigation : snuffing out the rule of law. [1997]
26. Tobacco smoke and the nonsmoker. 1988.

FIGURE 3   The First Ten Entries Displayed after an Internet Search on the Keyword SMOKING Using the Alta Vista Search Engine (68,911 "Documents" Retrieved)

1. Why Smoking Is Good For You
   The Web's only comedy site. From the people who brought you poverty, inflation, and the common cold. Updated weekly!
2. Phyllis Schlafly Column 1/22/97 — The Smoking Gun in the Medicaid Mystery
   Phyllis Schlafly January 8, 1997 column.

(continued)

FIGURE 3 (continued)

3. AIRSPACE Action on Smoking and Health
   AIRSPACE Action on Smoking and Health. Anti-tobacco billboard in
   California. On December 18, a set of documents subpoenaed for
   Minnesota's suit against . . .
4. The Association Between Smoking and Periodontitis
   The Association Between Smoking and Periodontitis. Dr. Steven
   Offenbacher. UNC-CH Dental Research Center. The Association
   Between Smoking and . . .
5. Moon Cloud Cigar Rests & Pipe Smoking Accessories
   HOME FURNISHINGS * GIFTS * ART * CLASSES. House of Swing Inc.
   began as a series of successful functional art shows designed to . . .
6. Re: quitting smoking—well trying anyway
   Re: quitting smoking—well trying anyway. [Follow Ups] [Post Followup]
   [The Stop Smoking Center Message Board] [FAQ] Posted by Carrie on
   August . . .
7. MSNBC — Test your smoking Quotient
   MSNBC—Test your smoking Quotient. [Follow Ups] [Post Followup]
   [The Stop Smoking Center Message Board] [FAQ] Posted by Matthew
   Kinney on . . .
8. All Natural Smoking Blends
   OPTICAL DILLUSIONS. SMOKING BLENDS. HERBA GHANI. High
   potency smoking herb consisting of a unique blend of imported organics
   cured with rare essential . . .
9. CoverIt All Weather Shelters, Smoking Shelters for the workplace, garages, gre
   CoverIt & GrowIt All Weather Shelters, Greenhouses, Carports, Instant
   Buildings, Instant Garages, Instant Hangars, Instant Greenhouses,
   Instant Workshops,
10. No Smoke Software to Quit and Prevent Smoking
    NO SMOKE for Windows is a unique computer-aided method to quit
    smoking using many video game elements. Effective for the adult who wants
    to quit or the

Word count: smoking: 875978

FIGURE 4 Display of Musical Works under a Subject Heading with Main
Entry Based on Authorship (i.e., Composer)

1. Beethoven, Ludwig van, 1770-1827.
   Symphonies, no. 1, op. 21, C major
2. Symphonies, no. 2, op. 36, D major
3. Symphonies, no. 3, op. 55, E flat major

FIGURE 4   (continued)

4.   Symphonies, no. 4, op. 60, B flat major
5.   Symphonies, no. 5, op. 67, C minor
6.   Bizet, Georges, 1838-1875.
     Symphonies, C major
7.   Borodin, Aleksandr Porfir'evich, 1833-1887.
     Symphonies, no. 2, B minor
8.   Dvorak, Antonin, 1841-1904.
     Symphonies, no. 1, C minor
9.   Symphonies, no. 2, op. 4, B flat major
10. Haydn, Joseph, 1732-1809.
     Symphonies, H. I, 6, D major
11. Ives, Charles, 1874-1954.
     Symphonies, no. 1
12. Mahler, Gustav, 1860-1911.
     Symphonies, no. 5, C# minor
13. Mozart, Wolfgang Amadeus, 1756-1791.
     Symphonies, K. 22, B flat major
14. Prokofiev, Sergey, 1891-1953.
     Symphonies, no. 1, op. 25, D major
15. Schubert, Franz, 1797-1828.
     Symphonies, D. 417, C minor
16. Tchaikovsky, Peter Ilich, 1840-1893.
     Symphonies, no. 1, op. 13, G minor

FIGURE 5   Display of Musical Works under a Subject Heading
             with Title Main Entry

1. Symphonie no. 1 op. 21 ; Symphonie no. 7 op. 92 [sound recording] / Ludwig van Beethoven
2. Symphony no. 1 / Charles Ives ; Three essays for orchestra / Samuel Barber [sound recording]
3. Symphony no. 1, in C major [sound recording] / Georges Bizet
4. Symphony no. 1, in C minor : The bells of Zlonice ; The hero's song : op. 111 [sound recording] / Dvorak
5. Symphony no. 2, in B flat major, op. 4 [sound recording] / Dvorak
6. Symphony no. 1, in D, op. 25 : Classical ; Symphony no. 4, op. 47/112 : revised 1947 version [sound recording] / Sergey Prokofiev
7. Symphony no. 1, in G minor, op. 13 (Winter dreams) [sound recording] / Tchaikovsky

(continued)

FIGURE 5   (continued)

8. Symphony no. 2, in B minor [sound recording] / Borodin

9. Symphony no. 2, in D major, op. 36 ; Overture Coriolan, op. 62 ; Overture Prometheus, op. 43 [sound recording] / Ludwig van Beethoven

10. Symphony no. 3, in E flat major, op. 55 (Eroica) [sound recording] / Ludwig van Beethoven

11. Symphony no. 4, in B flat, op. 60 ; Symphony no. 8, in F major, op. 93 [sound recording] / Ludwig van Beethoven

12. Symphony no. 4, in C minor, D. 417 (Tragic) ; Symphony no. 5, in B flat major, D. 485 [sound recording] / Franz Schubert

13. Symphony no. 5, in B flat major, K. 22 / Mozart

14. Symphony no. 5, in C minor, op. 67 [sound recording] / Ludwig van Beethoven

15. Symphony no. 5, in C sharp minor ; Symphony no. 10, in F sharp major [i.e., minor] [sound recording] / Gustav Mahler

16. Symphony no. 6, in D (1761) "Le matin" [sound recording] / Joseph Haydn

FIGURE 6   Potential Compressed Displays for Selected Works of Shakespeare and for Many Editions of a Particular Work (Macbeth)

Shakespeare, William, 1564-1616.

1. All's well that ends well.
2. Antony and Cleopatra.
3. As you like it.
4. Comedy of errors.
5. Coriolanus.
6. Cymbeline.
7. Hamlet.
8. Henry V.
9. Henry VI.
10. Macbeth.

When the user chooses line 10, for *Macbeth,* the following display could result:

Shakespeare, William, 1564-1616. Macbeth.

1. Editions of Macbeth.[7]
2. Other works related to Macbeth.[8]
3. Works about Macbeth.[9]

FIGURE 7 Potential Displays for Many Editions of a Particular Work (<u>Macbeth</u>), Created by Defining a Value for Performance in the Second Indicator Position of the MARC 21 7XX Fields

Shakespeare, William, 1564-1616. Macbeth.

1. Editions of Macbeth.[10]
2. Performances of Macbeth.
3. Other works related to Macbeth.[11]
4. Works about Macbeth.[12]

When the user chooses line 2, for performances of *Macbeth*, the following display could result:

1. Classic theatre. Macbeth. 1977.
2. Hallmark hall of fame. Macbeth (1954)
3. Hallmark hall of fame. Macbeth (1960)
4. Macbeth (1948)
5. Macbeth (1971)
6. Studio one. Macbeth. 1951.
7. Throne of blood. Akira Kurosawa's throne of blood. 1957.

Performances of would be for same main-entry sound and video-recordings (mere recordings); *films based on* would be for films (i.e., motion pictures and videorecordings) with related work-added entries for the preexisting works from which they were adapted.

If we take a musical example, it might look like this:

Mozart, Wolfgang Amadeus, 1756–1791. Zauberflöte.

1. Music scores[5]
2. Performances on sound recording[6]
3. Performances on videorecording
4. Films based on
5. Other related works
6. Works about

The main entry could also be used to develop compressed displays of the subparts of a work (see Figure 8).

Now that we have established the value of the main entry and demonstrated many of the useful things it does, we should consider the issue of how best to name works (using the main entry). It is very important to separate issues concerning the *form of name* we use for a work from issues concerning the *definition of work* (including *same work* and *related work,* covered previously). The film *Seven Samurai* has been released under three different titles: (1) *Seven Samurai,* (2) *Shichinin no samurai* (a transliteration of the Japanese script), and (3) *Magnificent Seven.* The question of whether to use a uniform title to bring together all of the editions of a work is different from the question of what that uniform title should be (e.g., whether it should be in the language of the library users, English in most of the United States, for example, or in the language of the country of origin of the work in question, Japanese, for example, for a Japanese film). A number of commentators have pointed out the possibility of developing international authority records that identify the language of each heading contained in them, allowing libraries to designate their own language forms as the preferred forms for display in their online public access catalogs (OPACs). This could potentially free us from the tyranny of language that led commentators like Eva Verona to oppose the use of uniform titles because her users didn't like having to deal with foreign languages. Allowing an English language–speaking population to search for works under their English-language titles, regardless of their titles in their countries of origin, would allow us to come closer to our principle of trying to enter authors and works under the names by which they are commonly known.

In cases in which two functions are performed to create a work of mixed responsibility, when is one of those functions predominant, such that the name of the person carrying out that function should be used to identify the work? And when are works of mixed authorship more appropriately identified and cited by title than by one of several authors of the work? Is Gerald Marks's name really essential for identifying and citing the song "All of Me"?

What about a work with two authors that is commonly known by both their names (such as Masters and Johnson)? Is there any way to use

FIGURE 8   Compressed Display of the Subparts of a Musical Work

Verdi, Giuseppe, 1813-1901.

1. Aida
2. Aroldo
3. Attila
4. Ballo in maschera
5. Don Carlos
6. Ernani
7. Falstaff
8. Forza del destino
9. Giorno di regno
10. Lombardi alla prima crociata
11. Luisa Miller
12. Macbeth
13. Messa da Requiem
14. Pezzi sacri
15. Rigoletto
16. Simon Boccanegra
17. Traviata
18. Trovatore

When line 18 is selected, the next display could appear as:

Verdi, Giuseppe, 1813-1901. Trovatore

1. Music scores
2. Performances on sound recording
3. Performances on videorecording
4. Films based on
5. Other related works
6. Works about
7. Parts:
   Ah! che la morte ognora
   Ah, si ben mio
   D'amor sull'ali rosee
   Deserto sulla terra
   Di quella pira
   Mal reggendo allaspro assalto
   Tacca la notte placida

system design solutions to ensure that a user search using two author names to identify a work can be assured of success? Will that user be able to recognize the work sought if it is identified using only the name of one of the authors (e.g., Masters, but not Johnson), if the search leads to the display of hundreds of records?

Why Haven't Lubetzky's Principles Been Carried Out in Our Catalogs?

There are actually three answers to this question. One is that cataloging budgets have been slashed, and few librarians are taught to catalog anymore (including at UCLA, which has dismantled the cataloging program founded by Lubetzky), because of an expectation on the part of library administrators and library school educators that any day now Bill Gates is going to come up with an intelligent assistant that will be able to catalog everything for us, without human intervention. Another answer to this question is that system design to support known-work searching in our OPACs has been so poor that catalogers have despaired of getting their carefully collocated work records displayed to users. And the third answer to this question is that our shared cataloging environment actually works *against* the sharing of the kind of authority work that is necessary to collocate works for our users.

Contrary to what the leaders of the profession seem to think, artificial intelligence is not the answer;[13] as one computer scientist puts it, "After fifty years of effort . . . it is now clear to all but a few diehards that [the] attempt to produce general intelligence [on the part of a computer] has failed. . . . The know-how that made up the background of common sense could not itself be represented by data structures made up of facts and rules."[14] Machines have had a particularly hard time *learning* natural language and *learning* how to do recognition tasks, such as recognizing the nature of the relationship between two entities. Not unexpectedly, efforts in our field to build expert systems have not been very successful. Hjerppe and Olander report on a project that built two expert systems for cataloging; they note that "much of the present cataloging process consists of 'instinctive' interpretation, based essentially on experiential learning from examples in an apprenticeship manner."[15] Among the number of interpretive acts they identify that are difficult for computers to carry out is "the recognition of an item as possibly being related to other item(s) and identifying such item(s)."[16] Humans can perform such recognition tasks nearly effortlessly, e.g.:

> This different name probably represents the same person.
>
> This different title probably represents the same work.
>
> This same name probably represents a different person.
>
> This same title probably represents a different work.

Recognition of the likelihood of a relationship can then trigger research to confirm or deny the existence of one.

What we need is not artificial intelligence, but rather human intelligence applied toward developing human-machine partnerships that maximize human intellectual input and minimize human drudgery. If catalogers did nothing but identify relationships all day long, they could accomplish much more work in a day than they do now on largely antiquated editing software in many different systems, few of which have been effectively designed to support cataloging work per se.

Another reason Lubetzky's work principle has not been carried out in our catalogs is that we have done a very bad job of both record design and system design for OPACs. Record design is embodied in the MARC 21 formats. In a sense, there is a format for author names and subject headings (authority format) and a format for particular editions of works (bibliographic format), but no specific format for works. Instead, authority records are occasionally adapted to represent works as well as authors and subjects, as in the case of name-title authority records for works entered under author and uniform title authority records for works entered under title. The most common situation is for a work to be represented *only* by the main entry on a bibliographic record, with no corresponding work authority record. Thus, when systems force users to choose between a search of authority records and a search of bibliographic records, as they always do, representation of the work, carried out as it is by both authority records and bibliographic records in conjunction, is imperfectly done no matter which choice the user makes.

System design failures are at work here, too. In general, OPACs are at their worst when it comes to helping a user find a work of which both author and title are known, probably still the most common search conducted in research libraries. Systems cannot seem to handle an identifier that sometimes occurs in two fields (e.g., 100 and 245) and sometimes in one field broken into subfields (e.g., 700 with a ǂt subfield) (see Figure 9).

FIGURE 9   Example of a Work Sometimes Identified by Two Fields and Sometimes by One

Work identified using two fields:

> 100 1_ ǂa Shakespeare, William, ǂd 1564-1616.
> 245 00 ǂa Macbeth.

Work identified using one field:

> 700 12 ǂa Shakespeare, William, ǂd 1564-1616. ǂt Macbeth.

Systems also cannot handle an identifier that sometimes consists of a uniform heading (that can be dynamically updated, e.g., 130) and sometimes consists of a transcribed field (that must be protected from dynamic updating, e.g., 245). I know of no existing OPACs that display all of these together effectively. They never offer users a search for a known work, and they often force the user to choose either author *or* title. For example, MELVYL (the University of California Web catalog site) offers the options of *Title, Author, Subject,* or *Power* searches on the initial search screen; DRA's Web catalog offers the search options of *Any word or words, Search by subject, Search by author, Search by title.*

Even when a combined author-title search is available, it tends to be treated as an expert or power search, and it tends to be done as a keyword within bibliographic record search, such that the authority file is not searched for name and title variants, and the only possible display is a display of bibliographic records in main-entry order. Thus, any work *added entries* that may have been retrieved will not be apparent in the display, and many false drops are produced, which can be difficult to differentiate on summary displays from works that contain the work sought, works about it, etc. For example, if a user performs a known-item name-title search for Arthur Miller's work entitled *Death of a Salesman,* the following are correctly retrieved:

Harshbarger, Karl.

The burning jungle : an analysis of Arthur Miller's Death of a salesman / Karl Harshbarger. — Washington : University Press of America, c1979.

SUBJECTS: 1. Miller, Arthur, 1915– Death of a salesman.

Miller, Arthur, 1915–

Death of a salesman : certain private conversations in two acts and a requiem / by Arthur Miller. — Harmondsworth, Eng. ; New York : Penguin, 1976.

Miller, Arthur, 1915–

The portable Arthur Miller / edited, and with an introduction by Harold Clurman. — New York : Viking Press, 1973, c1971.

CONTENTS: Death of a salesman — The crucible — Incident at Vichy — The price.

OTHER ENTRIES: 1. Miller, Arthur, 1915– Death of a salesman. 2. Miller, Arthur, 1915– Crucible ... [etc.]

The following false drop, however, might also be retrieved:

Berger, Brian.

Thomas Wolfe : the final journey / by Brian F. Berger ; with a remembrance by Edward M. **Miller.** — West Linn, Or. : Willamette River Press, 1984.

SUBJECTS: 1. Wolfe, Thomas, 1900-1938—Journeys—West (U.S.) 2. Wolfe, Thomas, 1900-1938—Last years and **death.** . . . [etc.]

Most OPAC summary displays for this search would look like this:

Search done: FIND NAME TITLE miller death

1. Berger, Brian. Thomas Wolfe : the final journey. 1984
2. Harshbarger, Karl. The burning jungle. c1979.
3. Miller, Arthur, 1915– Death of a salesman. 1976.
4. Miller, Arthur, 1915– The portable Arthur Miller. c1971.

Note also how retrieved records are not summarized as to whether they are editions of the work itself, related works, or works about the work, thus producing the unmanageably large results sets that plague

OPAC users. On the UCLA Libraries' OPAC, this search produces sixty-two results, many of which are false drops.

Bad record design and bad catalog design have dulled us to our mission to carry out the cataloging objectives. It is no wonder that even many catalogers have forgotten the potential value of main entries using uniform titles when necessary for carrying out the objectives of the catalog. Perhaps catalogs of the future will be able to demonstrate relationships in a more effective way. In the card catalog, the user could look in only a few predictable places. In the online catalog, the users have many more kinds of searching available, which makes it that much harder to ensure that they will, in fact, look at the main entry.

Another reason Lubetzky's work principle has not been carried out in our catalogs lies in the nature of our system of shared cataloging. To keep the costs of cataloging down, shared cataloging programs have been developed extensively in this country. Shared cataloging, however, can have the effect of working against the functions of the catalog. The products of shared cataloging are individual records, an atomized catalog, if you will; these atoms link to each other only when two records contain the same character strings in a normalized heading field.[17] Certainly, we share the creation of authority records, as well as bibliographic records. Yet, the creation of an authority record for a particular author or work does not automatically cause the form of that author's name or the uniform title for that work to be updated in every bibliographic record in which it appears in every catalog in the country. In fact, our national databases and many of our local systems are under very poor authority control. In subscribing to the shared cataloging effort, it could be argued that a cataloging department is taking on the responsibility for maintaining not just its local catalog, but a national database, and the Library of Congress's catalog as well. Maintaining three catalogs is more work than maintaining one. And even if those three are perfectly maintained, that does not take care of the problem of all the other local systems that are not updated when a heading is changed. If the term *information superhighway* can be translated to mean ubiquitous and cheap telecommunication, it could enable us to create a virtual single catalog that would be more like a coral reef built up by catalogers over time, rather than the current catalog model that resembles a cloud of atoms buzzing about, sometimes linking up when they should and sometimes not. Surely maintaining one catalog would be less expensive than maintaining thousands of catalogs, as we do now. We just need to work out a clever economic solution to the problem of how to pool our current resources and spend them on one shared catalog.

Of course, the idea of a single catalog is not a new one; each bibliographic database such as that of the Online Computer Library Center (OCLC) and the Research Libraries Information Network (RLIN) was meant to create a single catalog for many libraries (for that matter, from the time of Charles Jewett, various attempts have been made to create a single national catalog). It is certainly true that in some sense each national database was meant to form a single national catalog; the problem is that the emphasis was on creating atomized records, not on creating a catalog in which records were bound together by the demonstration of relationships between them; also, system design assumed as the primary purpose the creation of a warehouse of records from which "stock" could be ordered up using LCCNs, ISBNs, and the like as "stock numbers." The systems were never well designed to support direct user access. On OCLC, for example, it is still difficult to do searches that result in large retrievals; there are no effective displays of multiple headings (e.g., displays that link together the editions of a particular work), and displays of multiple bibliographic records are cumbersome, badly arranged (e.g., editions don't come together), and difficult to scan through.

I would like to suggest the following specifications for the ideal catalog system that would link editions together for users, no matter what their initial search might be. Please remember that the real problem is not the need for mechanical linking devices per se. They are readily available now through hypertext linking. The problem is to devise a method for creating one-to-many links that can be shared, that are immediately ubiquitous, and permanent.

1. The system would recognize the following six hierarchical levels: (1) superwork,[18] (2) work, (3) version, (4) edition, (5) near-equivalent,[19] and (6) copy.

2. A human operator would be able to point to two records and click on a type of relationship (e.g., same work, same version, different edition; or same work, same version, same edition, different near-equivalent).

   a. This action of recording a relationship need only be done once (that is, it would not need to be replicated in multiple databases).

   b. The recording of the relationship would be permanent (but editable).

   c. The recording of the relationship would be immediately ubiquitous, i.e., visible to all users, shared.

d. At each level of the tier that has levels below it, a textual label or citation form would be devised to identify or name the one entity, e.g., the superwork, work, version, edition, or near-equivalent, to which many subrecords can be linked. This label can be derived from the description of the entity, e.g., main entry (author and title, or title) for the work.

3. As long as local physical collections exist, users should be allowed to limit or prioritize their searches to items that are either locally held or readily available online and that are in particular formats, and they should have ready access to any call number, location, holdings, and circulation information needed to obtain the item or a particular volume or part of it.

Summary

One of Lubetzky's gifts to library users who seek particular works was his explication of the work principle, which has the potential to allow us to design OPACs that meet the cataloging objectives better than any catalogs we have ever seen before. The generations of library leaders that followed Lubetzky dropped the ball, however, and allowed the development of OPACs that impede the user who seeks particular works much more than the card catalog ever did. Perhaps it is time for a Renaissance of the work principle to lead the library catalog out of the Dark Ages that current library leadership have allowed to descend over it.

NOTES

1. Seymour Lubetzky, *Principles of Cataloging: Final Report, Phase I: Descriptive Cataloging* (Los Angeles: University of California Institute of Library Research, 1969), p. 52–53.

2. Joseph R. Matthews, Gary S. Lawrence, and Douglas K. Ferguson, eds., *Using Online Catalogs: A Nationwide Survey: A Report of a Study Sponsored by the Council on Library Resources* (New York: Neal-Shuman, 1983), 146.

3. The relationship is rather a special one, in which one work *depicts* another.

Our practice has probably not been consistent between considering this a subject relationship (6XX fields in the MARC 21 format) or a descriptive relationship (7XX fields in the MARC 21 format). Perhaps it needs definition as a separate type of relationship in its own right. For a much fuller discussion of this problem, see Sara Shatford, "Describing a Picture," *Cataloging & Classification Quarterly* 4, no. 4 (Summer 1984): 13–30.

4. Sherman Clarke and Jenni Rodda moderated a discussion on the Mona Lisa phenomenon at the 1997 conference of the Visual Resources Association.

5. Included here are records for scores with added entries for the work with second indicator 2 (meaning the work is contained within the work described by the retrieved record). One could break down the display by language, or include selections, vocal scores, librettos, etc. Another option would be to list these in the initial display.

6. Included here are records for sound recordings with added entries for the work with second indicator 2 (meaning the work is contained within the work described by the retrieved record).

7. Include here added entries for the work with second indicator 2 (MARC 21 format), indicating that they are contained in the work cataloged.

8. In the MARC 21 format, added entries for the work with second indicator 1 or blank.

9. In the MARC 21 format, 6XX fields contain subject-added entries for the work.

10. Include here added entries for the work with second indicator 2 (MARC 21 format), indicating that they are contained in the work cataloged.

11. In the MARC 21 format, added entries for the work with second indicator 1 or blank.

12. In the MARC 21 format, 6XX fields contain subject-added entries for the work.

13. See, for example, Hubert L. Dreyfus, *What Computers Still Can't Do: A Critique of Artificial Reason* (Cambridge, Mass.: MIT Press, 1992); James H. Fetzer, *Artificial Intelligence: Its Scope and Limits,* Studies in Cognitive Systems, vol. 4 (Dordrecht, Netherlands: Kluwer Academic Publishers, 1990); John Kelly, *Artificial Intelligence: A Modern Myth,* Ellis Horwood Series in Artificial Intelligence (New York: Ellis Horwood, 1993); Eric Sven Ristad, *The Language Complexity Game,* Artificial Intelligence (Cambridge, Mass.: MIT Press, 1993); Joseph F. Rychlak, *Artificial Intelligence*

and Human Reason: A Teleological Critique (New York: Columbia University Press, 1991).

14. Dreyfus, *What Computers Still Can't Do,* p. ix, xii.

15. Roland Hjerppe and Birgitta Olander, "Cataloging and Expert Systems: AACR2 as a Knowledge Base," *Journal of the American Society for Information Science* 40, no. 1 (Jan. 1989): 34.

16. Ibid., p. 35.

17. Character strings that are identical but not normalized can also link; problems arise, however, when the same character strings represent different entities, e.g., two different works that happen to have the same title. Here normalization can have the potential to differentiate two entities with the same character string, e.g., using qualifiers such as date of original publication or release, form (textbook versus play), publisher, etc.

18. *Superwork* is a concept that could be applied to works such as *Macbeth* that generate many spin-off works, such as various adaptations and film versions.

19. *Near-equivalent* is a concept that could be applied to copies in different physical formats, such as a microform copy of a particular edition of a particular work, and the text copied, or copies that differ only in distribution information, e.g., an edition (particular setting of the type) that has been issued by two different publishers or distributors in two different years with no change in the text.

8

Applying the Concept of the Work to New Environments

GREGORY H. LEAZER

Seymour Lubetzky stands out as a major cataloging theorist of the century. His work on cataloging simplification and the codification process and the way he shaped the debate on cataloging objectives and practices continues to be felt today. At UCLA he had a tremendous impact on his students and colleagues, and he continues to be an influential figure in the curriculum. I remember, as a master's student at Columbia University, how Lubetzky's writings provoked me: they gave weight to an activity I hadn't fully considered, allowed me to penetrate beyond the flurry of detail that is the bane of students beginning instruction in cataloging, and gave me a sense of purpose of cataloging. And it wasn't just me; my students today gravitate to his writings and cite them freely in their term papers in courses on cataloging and the organization of information. In many cases, I see the same development of understanding happening to them in the way that it happened to me, with Lubetzky's writings as the catalyst.

If I were to acknowledge Lubetzky for one thing, it would be for his concept of the work. Lubetzky outlined the objectives of the catalog in *Cataloging Rules and Principles* in 1953.[1] The first objective is the identification of individual bibliographic resources; the second objective is the "collocation" function, by which related works are brought together in the catalog. In "The Objectives of the Catalog," originally written in 1969, Lubetzky asks

> whether the objective of the catalog should be merely to tell an inquirer whether or not the library has the *particular book* he is looking for, or whether it should go beyond that and tell him also what other editions and translations—or other representations—of the *work* the library has so as to help him more effectively to determine whether the library has and what he needs to select what might best suit his purposes.[2]

In 1953 Lubetzky stated the objectives, in slightly different form:

> The second objective [of the catalog] is designed to enhance the utility and effectiveness of the catalog by requiring the cataloger also to relate the given work to the other works of the author and the other editions of the work. Thus the catalog will tell the inquirer not only whether or not a given work is in the library, but also what other editions or translations of the work the library has, and what other works of the author, so that he could select the edition most useful or suitable for his purposes, or another edition if the one wanted is not in the library.[3]

The concept of the work is the foundation for understanding the objectives of the catalog. The concept distinguishes the catalog from other bibliographical retrieval devices in its attempt to explicitly control works by assembling them under standardized forms of access points and by assembling all the various editions together in a single place.

Lubetzky's concept of the work has provoked a body of research continuing and even increasing in the present day. Wilson, in 1968, further strengthened the concept of the work, and introduced the concept of the bibliographic family.[4] Wilson also discussed the two objectives of the catalog in an essay in 1989.[5] Tillett, in her 1987 UCLA dissertation, examined the associations among bibliographic entities, and measured their incidence as expressed in the Library of Congress catalog.[6] Smiraglia, in his 1992 University of Chicago dissertation, further theorized the concept of the work, and developed a taxonomy of derivative bibliographic relationships.[7] He also measured the size and frequency of occurrence of bibliographic families from a sample drawn from the catalog of Georgetown University. I developed a model for the expression of bibliographic relationships in a library catalog in my 1993 dissertation,[8] and

Vellucci examined the relationships among musical works in her 1995 dissertation,[9] both at Columbia University. Yee examined the concept of the work as it applied to moving image resources in her 1993 dissertation,[10] and Carlyle investigated the work and collocation in her 1994 dissertation,[11] both at UCLA. Lubetzky's concept of the work has been at the foundation of a growing body of theoretical and empirical research that takes the form and function of the catalog as its primary concern, and seeks to utilize technology and reform cataloging codes to express bibliographic relationships more effectively. It is also important to note the prominence of the dissertation genre, indicating that a number of young scholars were inspired to research careers in part because of problems associated with the concept of the work.

Lubetzky's two objectives are occasionally called the item objective and the work objective: the first objective is to describe and identify items as "concrete entities"; the second objective is to control works. The work objective is not fully realized in contemporary catalogs. It would be done properly, as Wilson describes, by providing data elements that are proper for the description of works as intellectual or linguistic creations,[12] and as Smiraglia and Tillett imply, by modeling the network of associations that exist among works.[13]

How can we model the associations among works? Figure 1 is a directed graph of one such family. Work 1 is the progenitor work and has a successive derivation such as a second edition, Work 2. This work is translated in turn into two works, perhaps in different languages, Works 3 and 4. Finally, Work 3 is performed, perhaps read (or played if it is sheet music) and recorded, in Work 5.

A number of observations occur from this method of describing works. First, any work can potentially serve as a progenitor for one or more derivative works. Second, we call each of these nodes its own work, in a meaning that is slightly different from Lubetzky's meaning of the work—he would have called all of these works different editions of a work; the definition of the work used in this chapter describes each node as a separate work within a bibliographic family. Carlyle has also used the term "superwork" for these large sets of interrelated works.[14] Third, we can create a taxonomy of types of relationships among works and detect them as they occur. Finally, bibliographic families can potentially evolve in a complex, nonlinear way that is difficult to express in a simple linear fashion as is currently done with a single long alphabetical sequence of access points in the contemporary catalog.

Each work node in Figure 1 can be associated with one or more material expressions of that work, as seen in Figure 2. Here an item node consists of some type of document, broadly defined, including books, moving images, sound recordings, items within an archival collection, an electronic file, or an artifact—any material expression of information, typically a linguistic expression of human intellect, though we can perhaps be broader than that. An item can be thought of as a placeholder for a series of identical or near identical, mechanically or digitally reproduced, copies.

Work nodes are a way of aggregating identical (or near identical) items, perhaps separate print runs of a book, or different publishers' editions of a work, where the intellectual content of the two works is *perceived* as identical. I state "perceived" because it is important to acknowledge that the identity of a work in two separate items, or as two related works in two separate items, is the decision of the reader alone. The "Wicked Bible" provides a case. The 1631 edition of the Bible, published by Barker, is a standard Christian Bible of its day, with one notable exception: it is missing the word "not" in the seventh

FIGURE 1   Relationships among Works

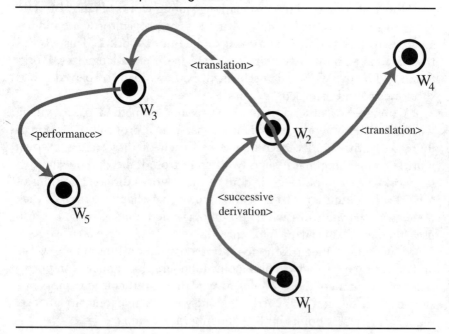

commandment, yielding "Thou shalt commit adultery." Does the exception of a single word yield a new work? Most people probably are already aware of the intended meaning and might not even notice the absence of the word. But we can, in theory at least, imagine a naive reader who accepts this edition as holy word, and thus lives a life that would be very different than if he or she had a different Bible—a different work. If such a person never existed, certainly the difference between works was not lost on Barker, who was given a "deep fine" of £300.[15] Thus for everyone but those levying or paying a fine, the two works could be considered as equivalent, and thus aggregated as a single work node with two items associated with it. But the practical consequence for the publisher was that these are two separate works, highly related, and the work node for the Wicked Bible would have only a single item node attached to it. There may be as yet undiscovered empirical evidence that would allow us to make the decision of textual identity on behalf of the reader, based on an investigation of the methods used by

FIGURE 2 Completed Bibliographic Family

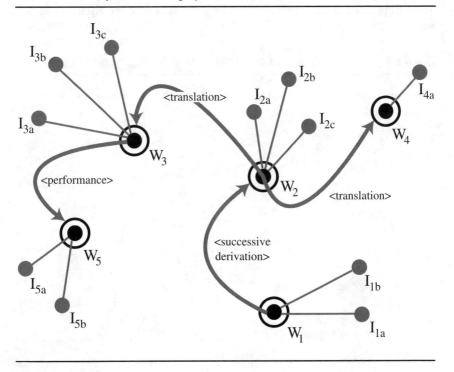

readers to make decisions regarding the substitution of one text for another. Ultimately, however, the final arbiter of the identity of a work is the individual reader who decides for himself or herself when two works are different or equivalent.

A relationship between two works carries a weight. We can scale the weight from zero (where there is no relationship between two works) to one (where two works are seen as identical). An example updated from Leazer and Smiraglia demonstrates this: Figure 3 is a representation of the *Alphabetical Biographical Catalog*, a family with one or two works, and two items.[16] This case was chosen because of the almost certain identical textual content of the two works. The first work is contained in a 244-page book, published in 1933. The second work is a photographic (microfilm) reproduction of the book. We could describe this as one work with two items, and in fact many people would do so. We can also describe it as two works, however, with a high degree of overlap with a weight of .95 or higher. We can consider this as two works because of the simple fact of the material form of the item: many people refuse to use microfilm, or lack the equipment. Thus for them, the two are different works because one is not even accessible to them.

FIGURE 3   Directed Graph of the <u>Alphabetical Biographical Catalog</u>

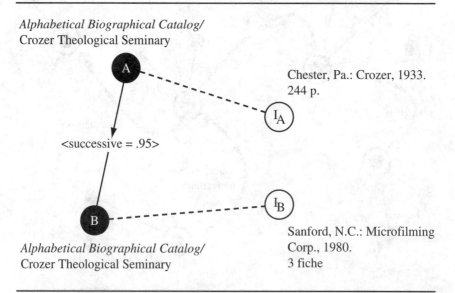

Alphabetical Biographical Catalog/
Crozer Theological Seminary

Chester, Pa.: Crozer, 1933.
244 p.

I_A

<successive = .95>

I_B

B

Alphabetical Biographical Catalog/
Crozer Theological Seminary

Sanford, N.C.: Microfilming
Corp., 1980.
3 fiche

The .95 weight of the successive relationship between the two works is a measure of the similarity of textual content. The person describing this family considers identical textual content (though leaving the possibility that slight differences might exist) to mean that most people would interpret these works as a single work. The microfilm, however, is literally viewed through a lens in ways that certainly modify the reception of the work, and we cannot claim that the two works are purely identical.

Many works do not exist as members in bibliographic families with derivative members. Approximately one-half to two-thirds of all works share no derivative associations. Smiraglia's 1992 dissertation showed that approximately half of all works in Georgetown University's libraries did exist in bibliographic families or, more precisely, shared a derivative bibliographic relationship and thus existed in a bibliographic family with more than one member.[17] Smiraglia constituted his bibliographic families, as mentioned previously, through an examination of national bibliographic utilities. Smiraglia and Leazer replicated this research study in a sample of works drawn from the OCLC Online Computer Library Center's WorldCat (a union catalog of several hundred libraries located primarily in the United States) and found that approximately one-third of such works existed in bibliographic families.[18]

Family size is another important descriptive attribute of bibliographic families. Smiraglia found a mean of 4.7 members per bibliographic family, with a total family size ranging from 1 to 217 members. The mean size for bibliographic families with size greater than or equal to two (i.e., a family exhibiting at least one derivative relationship) was 8.4 members.[19] The results from Smiraglia and Leazer are shown in Table 1. Thus, family size varies considerably, with most families being small, but some families being quite large. The article contains illustrations of bibliographic families over a range of sizes.

Several studies have also attempted to associate descriptive characteristics, such as a progenitor's age, form, or genre with the incidence of bibliographic relationships. The age of the progenitor work is the only attribute clearly shown to correlate with the size of a bibliographic family, but it does so only weakly. Smiraglia and Leazer found, for example, that the average bibliographic family starts out with 1.4 members and adds 1.2 new members every 100 years. Age accounts for only 3.7 percent of the variation in the size of bibliographic families. While such measures are statistically significant, they are so low as to be unimportant.[20]

TABLE 1   Number of Members in a Bibliographic Family

Family Size	Number of Cases	Percent of All Families	Margin of Error (95% confidence)	Percent of Families with Size > 1	Margin of Error (95% confidence)
1	333	69.8%	± 4.1%	—	—
2	77	16.1%	± 3.3%	53.5%	± 8.1%
3	24	5.0%	± 2.0%	16.7%	± 3.7%
4	13	2.7%	± 1.5%	9.0%	± 2.6%
5	13	2.7%	± 1.5%	9.0%	± 2.6%
6	7	1.5%	± 1.1%	4.9%	± 2.0%
7	4	0.8%	± 0.8%	2.8%	± 1.5%
8	1	0.2%	± 0.4%	0.7%	± 0.7%
9	1	0.2%	± 0.4%	0.7%	± 0.7%
10	1	0.2%	± 0.4%	0.7%	± 0.7%
12	1	0.2%	± 0.4%	0.7%	± 0.7%
13	1	0.2%	± 0.4%	0.7%	± 0.7%
45	1	0.2%	± 0.4%	0.7%	± 0.7%
TOTAL	477	100%		100%	
Mean		1.77		3.54	
Standard deviation		2.48		4.00	

Missing cases = 0

SOURCE: Richard P. Smiraglia and Gregory H. Leazer, "Derivative Bibliographic Relationships: The Work Relationship in a Global Bibliographic Database," *Journal of the American Society for Information Science* 50 (1999): 499.

Growing Complexity

Lubetzky inherited a morass of cataloging codes that had proliferated rules without reason. He also inherited the basics for his concept of the work, a concept he further developed and turned into the key that would help solve the midcentury crisis in cataloging. In fact, the first modern catalog distinguished itself from other forms of bibliography such as indexes and inventory lists by virtue of the fact that it was a collocating device—it alone attempted to gather together various related works into a single place in the catalog. Anthony Panizzi's work in the 1840s at the British Museum and his ninety-one rules for the construction of a catalog are widely acknowledged as the first appearance of the modern catalog.[21] But why should the catalog, based on early conceptions of the work, appear at that time? Quoting Chartier at length:

How did people in Western Europe between the end of the Middle Ages and the eighteenth century attempt to master the enormously increased number of texts that first the manuscript book and then print put into circulation? Inventorying titles, categorizing works, and attributing texts were all operations that made it possible to set the world of the written world in order. Our own age is the direct heir of this immense effort motivated by anxiety.[22]

Chartier's focus is on conceptual apparatuses such as the establishment of reading practices. The same anxiety, however, is still present in the writing of Joseph Henry, the first secretary of the Smithsonian Institution and a leading scientist of his day. Writing in the mid-nineteenth century, Henry states:

It is estimated that about twenty thousand volumes, including pamphlets, purporting to be additions to the sum of human knowledge, are published annually; and unless this mass be properly arranged, and the means furnished by which its contents may be ascertained, literature and science will be overwhelmed by their own unwieldy bulk. The pile will begin to totter under its own weight, and all the additions we may heap upon it will tend to add to the extension of the base, without increasing the elevation and dignity of the edifice.[23]

Part of Panizzi's contribution was a realization that the bibliographic universe was not simply getting larger, it was getting more complex. Writing to the chairman of the Royal Commission appointed to investigate the construction of the catalog at the British Museum, Panizzi provides several examples of difficulties in identifying, describing, and collocating various related works.[24] Panizzi describes books containing independent works of commentary published without adequate identification on the various works on the title page, the problem of anthologies, inconsistent forms of names, etc., all problems associated with complexity within the bibliographic family.

It is tempting to think of the catalog as an inevitable solution to the problem of growing complexity in the bibliographic universe. The catalog can be described as a case study that occurred during the "control revolution," a term used by Beniger.[25] According to Beniger, several changes occurred in the United States during the late nineteenth century. The demands of newly established industrial production and concomitant national (and international) markets, power production, and the development of large-scale technical systems such as railroads and telegraphy posed problems of detail that exceeded the ability of any one human to plan and control these systems. This period of time in the United States saw several developments that led to requirements for the systematic organization of knowledge, including the establishment of more libraries, and universities founded on the German research university model (such as Johns Hopkins University in 1876). A "new structure of scholarly and scientific activity was clearly worked out [during this period, . . . and] established itself as the controlling pattern of American intellectual life."[26] These developments led as well to the creation of specialized professions, with their concomitant requirements for access to published information.[27] All of these changes led to increased publishing and larger, more complex library collections.[28]

National literature production was of such number that no one person could know of, much less read or understand, the breadth of publishing being produced each year. The same problem applied to library collections, where the growth of collections increased so that no one person could have the detailed knowledge required to retrieve items from the collection. This anxiety was spurred on, in part, by evolving textual identity. In fact, the collocation achieved by the catalog was in part a way to reduce the cardinality of publications by aggregating individual books into larger conglomerate work units, and also provided a mechanism for placing individual works into the interpretive and contextual framework of the bibliographic family.

Complexity was also present because members of bibliographic families might be distributed over multiple collections, belonging to different libraries. National union catalogs were conceived as a solution to the problem of distributed resources right in the beginning of the nineteenth-century American information explosion. The Committee on Organization at the Smithsonian Institution proposed that the Smithsonian "become a centre of literary and bibliographical reference for the entire country . . . to procure catalogs of all the important works or bibliography so that they might be consulted by the scholar, the student, the author, the historian, from every section of the Union, and . . . to inform them whether any works they may desire to examine are to be found in the United States; and if so in what library . . ."[29]

In 1853, Charles Coffin Jewett, the librarian at the Smithsonian Institution, proposed to publish a union catalog of all the libraries in the country. Such a union catalog did not come into being at that point, but did in 1901 when the Library of Congress began to both collect and distribute bibliographic data in card form. This system allowed people to search multiple collections simultaneously, without prior knowledge of the existence of a particular library or its collection. The construction of large union catalogs was facilitated by wide-scale adherence to cataloging standards, which sought to control textual variation such as those found within bibliographic families.

Assembling the members of bibliographic families in this environment was accomplished by using systematic and standardized access points, and this solution remains with us today, though as Carlyle's dissertation research indicates, success has not been total in accomplishing this task.[30] When standardized descriptions of resources are brought together and assembled into coherent units in a single union catalog, and paired with document delivery mechanisms, however, the resulting system provides the means to search a single virtual collection, distributed across multiple libraries. Thus, a single coherent view was created over a growing, evolving mass of materials.

The recognition that members of bibliographic families are likely to be distributed across multiple collections is an important contribution of Smiraglia's study.[31] By exhaustively studying the many collections present in either one of two national union catalogs, Smiraglia recognized that in most situations no one single library typically endeavors to collect all the members of a bibliographic family—libraries sample from families and choose representative members. For the library user, however, the most appropriate member of a bibliographic family might not be present, and the means for indicating the existence of alternative or complementary works, such as criticisms and reviews, has yet to be established. The current research efforts on catalogs, the work, and bibliographic families implicitly acknowledges the failure of the status quo—either our solutions to date are inadequate or the problems related to the complexity and distribution of bibliographic families are getting worse.

In fact, the answer is both: contemporary technology is underutilized in the present-day catalog and limits the effectiveness and the benefits of library service. Panizzi, Jewett, and Lubetzky are major players in what is amounting, however, to be a 150-year (and longer) research problem on the development of optimal bibliographic retrieval systems. Current-day solutions are based on 100-year-old technologies and have not yet received the substantial rethinking that is required for today's digital environment.

Growing complexity in the body of recorded knowledge is placing more strain on already overburdened cataloging systems. The creation of new digital technologies is resulting in yet another of our many information explosions. What is unique to this explosion, however, is that we are faced with digital resources that are much easier to proliferate through copying. Exacerbating this problem is the fact that the digital information resources are easier to change as well, either through the direct application of human intellect, such as in the traditional case of revising a document for a new edition, or also through the application of automated processes such as computer-based algorithms to these resources, resulting in new informational content—added-value information products as the jargon goes. The fixity of paper-based forms of communication and the fluidity of electronic forms should not be viewed in absolute terms, as Levy points out,[32] though we are likely to have "a lot more variants of previously existing materials."[33] The creation of digital libraries is a response to a new crisis in control: the proliferation of digital resources. Thus, complexity is the result of growth—the sheer numbers of resources that exist in digital form—and is also the result of the accelerating pace of mutation—information resources will evolve and spawn derivative members faster than traditional print.

Complexity is also a felt problem as the number and types of collections of individual resources continue to grow. Scholarship never limited itself to the perusal of books, and modern scholarship, especially the interdisciplinary type, increasingly requires access to resources typically found not only in libraries, but also in museums of diverse types, archives, and on computer networks. The digital revolution in general and the development of the Internet in particular provide the means of access to these diverse collections. The various members of bibliographic families are found in all of these diverse types of collections, but the problem of integrating collections of various types is a paramount problem. The integration of traditional and digital library collections, described in Levy and Marshall as a primary goal of digital library research,[34] is but one component of a larger effort aimed at the integration of collections of even more diverse types.

The problem is shown schematically in Figure 4. Diverse types of users now have access to diverse types of collections through a single source. And just as on the Internet no one knows that you are a dog, no one need know whether a resource accessed over the Internet belongs to a public or university library, a digital library belonging to a professional association or publisher, a museum collection, a subject bibliography published by a commercial entity and licensed to a university, or a

FIGURE 4   Distributed and Diverse Collections

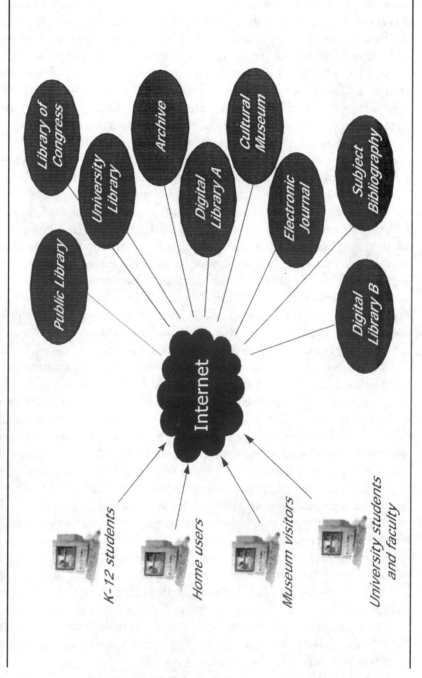

freely available electronic journal. The problem is providing a "coherent, consistent view of as many of these repositories as possible."[35]

Since the turn of the century, the integration of collections was generally limited to the formation of union catalogs where libraries aggregated their bibliographic records into a single catalog, a solution that grew to include national bibliographic utilities, such as the OCLC. This solution, however, failed to integrate the many library resources that were not described in the catalog. The long-expected combination of catalogs and bibliographies (described, for example, by Buckland[36]) has been stalled. Library catalogs have integrated information on archival collections through a modification of machine-readable cataloging (MARC) standards. The inclusion of diverse types of resources under the control of the library catalog has only been accomplished through adhering to a strict set of standards, including the *USMARC Format for Bibliographic Data*.[37] This is a "tight-coupling" solution to the integration of collections: strong adherence to highly specified national standards that require a professional education to implement.

The growing diversity of collections including digital library collections has put an end to the initial promise of the integration of other nonlibrary collections under the control of the catalog. In fact, recent developments in the archival community, such as the creation of the Encoded Archival Description (EAD), are symptoms of an unraveling of the library-archival partnership accomplished through the tight-coupling approach. The failure to integrate bibliography and abstracting tools into the catalog, the development of new archival standards, and emerging ad hoc solutions for the control of digital resources (the Internet search engine and idiosyncratic digital library retrieval systems) demand a new approach to the problem of integrating these collections. Such solutions for integrating diverse types of collections will likewise be ad hoc and idiosyncratic, driven by the requirements of loosely defined professional or disciplinary groupings rather than the requirements of a national or global clientele. These solutions will seek to integrate collections not through using a single standard deployed at member institutions, but rather through a loose coupling of individual systems.[38] A loose-coupling approach will typically work by grouping data elements from diverse collections and declaring them equivalent. In fact, mapping the elements of various standards to each other through a "crosswalk" has already emerged as a principle method of metadata integration research.

A hypothetical scenario best illustrates how an individual user might cope with these problems. Assume a searcher is looking for the song "This Land Is Your Land." The user, at home, wants to hear it and read the lyrics. Nowadays, the searcher would likely start with a relatively focused search, searching a collection he or she thinks might hold the item. The user would then be limited by the likely small number of items held within that collection, and if the collection is well chosen, then this is no problem. In the future as the number of collections expands, it is less likely that the user will select or even have knowledge of the most appropriate collection to search. As different types of collections become integrated, the user will cast a comparatively broader net. Such a user might enter the same query, e.g., "find title=this land is your land," but potentially retrieve thousands of hits out of hundreds of collections. The search scenario of the future has been described as one of specialized software in the form of search agents scouring multiple collections simultaneously, and bringing back all matched hits. This is already the problem that end users face when they search the Research Libraries Group's RLIN database, receiving a jumble of a response set with no clear clues on how the individual items might be the same, different, or related. How does the user select the most appropriate manifestation from this morass?

One solution to the problem of providing a coherent view of diverse collections is to finally implement the vision of Lubetzky and provide control over bibliographic families. As mentioned, bibliographic families are distributed across multiple collections of various types. By aggregating works that contain the same item, we would reduce the number of individual records the searcher is required to peruse in the retrieval set. By relating works to each other, we could provide a contextual framework that would allow the user to select the most appropriate work within the bibliographic family, indicating, for example, which work is an original sound recording, which is a contemporary interpretation of the song, and which is a simple transcription of the lyrics, without music. And bibliographic relationships, expressed as hypertextual links, would provide the means for users to navigate seamlessly among various collections.

Lubetzky, along with his precursors, provided us with a sophisticated concept of the work, a vision of the uses and functions of bibliographic retrieval systems. His ideas were not self-evident; as proof of this we can simply see that no other system, including other cataloglike systems such as subject bibliographies and abstracting tools, provides the sophisticated control over works such as he described for the library catalog. It is now our responsibility to advance this research, further elucidate the concept of the bibliographic work, and put it into effective practice in our retrieval systems. More than fifty years after Lubetzky first began laboring on this topic, the concept of the work will help us design systems in response to problems that are just beginning to emerge.

NOTES

1. Seymour Lubetzky, *Cataloging Rules and Principles: A Critique of the A.L.A. Rules for Entry and a Proposed Design for Their Revision* (Washington, D.C.: Library of Congress, 1953; reprint, High Wycombe, England: Published for the College of Librarianship, Wales, by University Microfilms, 1970).

2. Seymour Lubetzky, "The Objectives of the Catalog," in *Foundations of Cataloging: A Sourcebook,* ed. Michael Carpenter and Elaine Svenonius (Littleton, Colo.: Libraries Unlimited, 1985), p. 190 (originally published 1969).

3. Lubetzky, *Cataloging Rules and Principles,* p. 54.

4. Patrick Wilson, *Two Kinds of Power: An Essay on Bibliographical Control* (Berkeley, Calif.: University of California Press, 1968).

5. Patrick Wilson, "The Second Objective," in *The Conceptual Foundations of Descriptive Cataloging,* ed. Elaine Svenonius (San Diego, Calif.: Academic Press, 1989), p. 5–16.

6. Barbara A. Tillett, "Bibliographic Relationships: Toward a Conceptual Structure of Bibliographic Information Used in Cataloging" (Ph.D. diss., University of California, Los Angeles, 1987).

7. Richard P. Smiraglia, "Authority Control and the Extent of Derivative Bibliographic Relationships" (Ph.D. diss., University of Chicago, 1992).

8. Gregory H. Leazer, "A Conceptual Plan for the Description and Control of Bibliographic Works" (Ph.D. diss., Columbia University, 1993).

9. Sherry L. Vellucci, "Bibliographic Relationships among Musical Bibliographic Entities: A Conceptual Analysis of Music Represented in a Library Catalog with a Taxonomy of the Relationships Discovered" (Ph.D. diss., Columbia University, 1995).

10. Martha M. Yee, "Moving Image Works and Manifestations" (Ph.D. diss., University of California, Los Angeles, 1993).

11. Allyson Carlyle, "The Second Objective of the Catalog: An Evaluation of Collocation in Online Catalog Displays" (Ph.D. diss., University of California, Los Angeles, 1994).

12. Wilson, "The Second Objective," p. 9.

13. Smiraglia, "Authority Control"; Tillett, "Bibliographic Relationships."

14. Allyson Carlyle, "Ordering Author and Work Records: An Evaluation of Collocation in Online Catalog Displays," *Journal of the American Society for Information Science* 47 (1996): 538–54.

15. A. S. Herbert, *Historical Catalogue of Printed Editions of the English Bible: 1525–1961* (New York: American Bible Society, 1968), p. 162 (revised and expanded from the edition of T. H. Darlow and H. F. Moule, 1903).

16. Gregory H. Leazer and Richard P. Smiraglia, "Bibliographic Families in the Library Catalog: A Qualitative Analysis and Grounded Theory," *Library Resources & Technical Services* 43 (1999): 191–212.

17. Smiraglia, "Authority Control," p. 60.

18. Richard P. Smiraglia and Gregory H. Leazer, "Derivative Bibliographic Relationships: The Work Relationship in a Global Bibliographic Database," *Journal of the American Society for Information Science* 50 (1999): 493–504.

19. Smiraglia, "Authority Control," p. 74.

20. Smiraglia and Leazer, "Derivative Bibliographic Relationships," p. 501.

21. Anthony Panizzi, "Rules for the Compilation of the Catalogue," in *Foundations of Cataloging: A Sourcebook,* ed. Michael Carpenter and Elaine Svenonius (Littleton, Colo.: Libraries Unlimited, 1985), p. 3–17 (originally published 1841); see also "Mr. Panizzi to the Right Hon. The Earl of Ellesmere—British Museum, January 29, 1848," in *Foundations of Cataloging,* p. 18–47 (originally published 1848).

22. Roger Chartier, *The Order of Books: Readers, Authors and Libraries in Europe between the Fourteenth and Eighteenth Centuries,* trans. Lydia G. Cochrane (Cambridge, U.K.: Polity Press, 1994), p. viii.

23. Smithsonian Institution, *Annual Report of the Board of Regents, 1851* (Washington, D.C.: A. Boyd Hamilton, 1852), p. 22.

24. Panizzi, "Mr. Panizzi to the Right Hon. The Earl of Ellesmere," p. 19 ff.

25. James R. Beniger, *The Control Revolution: Technological and Economic Origins of the Information Society* (Cambridge, Mass.: Harvard University Press, 1986).

26. Arthur E. Bestor, Jr., "The Transformation of American Scholarship, 1875–1917," *Library Quarterly* 23 (1953): 168.

27. John Higham, "The Matrix of Specialization," in *The Organization of Knowledge in Modern America, 1860–1920,* ed. A. Oleson and J. Voss (Baltimore: Johns Hopkins University Press, 1979), p. 3–18.

28. Hendrik Edelman and G. Marvin Tatum, Jr., "The Development of Collections in American University Libraries," *College & Research Libraries* 37 (1976): 222–45.

29. Alphonse F. Trezza, "Library Cooperative Systems," in *ALA World Encyclopedia of Library and Information Services,* 2nd ed., ed. Robert Wedgeworth (Chicago: American Library Association, 1986), p. 472.

30. Carlyle, "The Second Objective of the Catalog."

31. Smiraglia, "Authority Control."

32. David M. Levy, "Fixed or Fluid? Document Stability and New Media," in *ACM European Conference on Hypermedia Technology 1994 Proceedings, ECHT 94, Edinburgh, UK, 18–23 Sept. 1994* (New York: Association for Computing Machinery, 1994), p. 24–31.

33. David M. Levy, "Naming the Namable: Names, Versions, and Document Identity in a Networked Environment," in *Filling the Pipeline and Paying the Piper: Proceedings of the Fourth Symposium,* ed. Ann Okerson (Washington, D.C.: Assn. of Research Libraries, 1995), p. 157.

34. David M. Levy and Catherine C. Marshall, "Going Digital: A Look at Assumptions Underlying Digital Libraries," *Communications of the ACM* 38, no. 4 (April 1995): 82.

35. Clifford Lynch and Hector Garcia-Molina, "Interoperability, Scaling, and the Digital Libraries Research Agenda: A Report on the May 18–19, 1995 IITA Digital Libraries Workshop," available from <http://www.ccic.gov/pubs/iita-dlw/main.html> (accessed 24 May 1999).

36. Michael K. Buckland, "Bibliography, Library Records, and the Redefinition of the Library Catalog," *Library Resources & Technical Services* 32 (1988): 299–311.

37. Network Development and MARC Standards Office, *USMARC Format for Bibliographic Data: Including Guidelines for Content Designation* (Washington, D.C.: Cataloging Distribution Service, Library of Congress, 1992).

38. Cheng Hian Goh, S. E. Madnick, and M. D. Siegel, "Context Interchange: Overcoming the Challenges of Large-Scale Interoperable Database Systems in a Dynamic Environment," in *CIKM 94: Proceedings of the Third International Conference on Information and Knowledge Management, Gaithersburg, MD, USA, 28 Nov.–2 Dec. 1994,* ed. N. R. Adam, B. K. Bhargava, and Y. Yesha (New York: ACM, 1994), p. 337–46.

The Future
of Cataloging

9

The Ideology and Technology of Cataloging at the End of the Millennium

MAURICE J. FREEDMAN

One should begin with the fundamental conditions from which the ideology of cataloging emanates. These conditions are simple. They have not changed for centuries. There are two basic conditions upon which cataloging theory and rules are based.

The first condition is that the names by which people identify themselves and by which others identify them may, and frequently do, vary.

The second condition is that the names by which the representations, translations, editions, etc., of a work are identified may, and frequently do, vary.

Neither the technology, events, nor anything else present at the end of the millennium has changed these fundamental conditions. In recognition of these apparently permanent conditions, the great thinkers who developed the Anglo-American cataloging ideology articulated the functions of the alphabetic catalog.

First, the catalog is to facilitate the user's finding a particular publication in the library.

Second, the catalog should relate and present to the user all of the works of a given author and all of the representations of a given work.

These functions clearly respond to the variability in the way people and representations of works are identified. These theorists have a simple message. Whatever the codes or rules, they must be directed to the goals of:

1. identifying a particular publication; and
2. identifying all of the works of a given author, and all of the editions, translations, and other representations of a given work.

The only alternative is *not* to present the user with all of the versions of a work and all of the works of an author. To date, no one has argued for the elimination of these functions, although an examination of today's online catalogs, in many instances, would reflect the contrary.

Knowing these are the functions of the catalog, how are they to be fulfilled?

Seymour Lubetzky has articulated the notion of *main entry* as the instrumentality by which the catalog's functions are achieved. Knowing full well that any expression of *main entry* will be found faulty by The Master, let us proceed, albeit imperfectly, with the following characterization:

The *main entry* identifies a given publication as the representation of a particular work by a particular author. It is incumbent on the cataloger to demonstrate the relatedness of given books, translations, editions, etc., to a given work; to establish the particularity of an author; and to link to each other or demonstrate the various ways in which the author has been identified.

Over time such devices as *see* and *see also* references and *uniform titles* have been created to help achieve the requirements of the main entry.

Having established this conceptual framework for the cataloging enterprise, Lubetzky then turns the job over to the worker bees to do the work of formulating cataloging codes and the myriad rules that comprise them. The codes serve to establish a set of rules that satisfy the demands of the main entry.

The real challenge is to develop rules within this framework that adequately address the variability, idiosyncrasies, novelty, and everything else that constitutes the forms of human, corporate, or other expression. The codes and their rules provide a basis for decision making by the catalogers to ensure that the records that they create will be part of a coherent whole, an organized body of information, the alphabetic catalog.

What from the past cataloging codes should be included in and excluded from future codes? Is the word *cataloging* passé?

I shall not offer a critique of the catalog codes on a rule-by-rule basis. Also, I shall not offer any specifics regarding what of the old codes should or shouldn't be included in the new codes. I leave that to the catalogers and the cataloging rule makers, again those indefatigable workers who catalog or supervise cataloging on a day-to-day basis.

I shall not, however, shrink from the question. Being an administrator or teacher for most of one's career and not a cataloger in no way absolves one from responding to such primary issues. On the other hand, being a practicing cataloger in no way entails that such an individual has any understanding of the conceptual foundations of the catalog and the ideology upon which it is based. Such an understanding is uncommon in U.S. catalog departments. The memorized (and usually quickly forgotten) objects of Charles Cutter recede into the past. There are too many catalogers who neither know who Seymour Lubetzky is nor have an appreciation for the conceptual framework he established and upon which their daily labors are based.

My general answer to the question, Is cataloging passé? follows from this syllogism:

A. The cataloging codes endeavor to provide rules that will enable the cataloger to establish bibliographic records for the seemingly infinite variety of materials and information that are presented to the cataloger for entry into a coherent body of records called the alphabetic catalog.

B. Nothing has occurred to change the fundamental conditions of variability that provided this premise from which the cataloging ideology and consequent codes have proceeded.

C. Therefore, my simple view is that what is in the current code that is deficient and can be improved should be fixed or excluded from the new codes. Should another genius like Seymour Lubetzky come along and do another *Is this rule necessary?* for the current code, any resultant rubble should be cleared away and what is necessary for the new code should be included.

I will leave to my Michael colleagues, Messrs. Carpenter and Malinconico, two people capable of endeavoring such an inquiry, the Augean task of such an analysis of the work of a third Michael, Mr. Gorman, the editor of the *Anglo-American Cataloguing Rules,* second edition.

Where the code will necessarily have to adapt is in its accommodation of new or variant forms of information.

To the extent that new forms of material present themselves—there were no websites at the time AACR2 was created—there may have to be guidance for the cataloger. How does one catalog a website? Should a website be cataloged? Such sites tend not to be static and the information contained there can and usually does change frequently. This tends not to be the case with the materials that physically reside in the library.

Even though websites do not physically reside in a library in the manner of today's library collections, the librarian wants to provide access to websites that have information that is of interest or utility to today's library user. Through the Internet, a user can be anywhere in the world and access any library's Web catalog, as well as any other information to which the librarian chooses to point or to include in the given catalog, such as (1) URLs (universal resource locators), (2) electronic text versions of publications, and (3) updates of such publications as guidebooks.

Thus, what is different is that before only materials *in* the library were represented in the alphabetic catalog; today, the Web catalog points beyond the library's holdings to electronic information residing in cyberspace.

I will not begin to explore the intricacies and variability of websites in relation to authorship, content, metadata, or anything else that already has created a cottage industry for those inclined to examine such issues.

One solution I suggest is simple regarding the treatment of websites and the catalog, but it requires an authority control system that rigorously links authority records to those bibliographic records in which they appear. Assuming such a system, I would have the cataloger embed given URL(s) in the related authority record.

In that way, for every cataloging record in which "Sinatra, Frank, 1915– " appears as an "author" or "subject," there also will be presented to the user the URL <http://www.Blue-Eyes.com> and any other websites substantially devoted to Sinatra that the cataloger chose to include.

The benefit of embedding the URL in the authority record is that the cataloger does not have to enter manually the URL into each Sinatra catalog record. And if the website disappears or its URL changes, all the cataloger need do is remove or change the URL in the authority record. The details of devising the software to accomplish this can be worked out. The strategy is sound and it will result in the same productivity and quality enhancements that machine-based authority-control systems introduced when implemented.

At present, librarians all over the country are doing far more work than is necessary to get URLs entered into catalog records, while having much less control over those entries when it comes to changing or removing those same URLs from the catalog records in which they have been inserted.

To be explicit, catalogers are entering manually the URL in the MARC field designated for URLs. But if there were ten books and forty recordings by and about Sinatra in the library's collection, the cataloger would have to enter that URL fifty times.

Once again, the brilliance of the authority-control system developed at the New York Public Library is demonstrated. And close to thirty years after its implementation at the NYPL, the functionality of authority control is finding its way into the turnkey systems being installed in libraries around the country.[1]

On a related point, OCLC Online Computer Library Center, certainly as represented by the writings of its founder, Frederick G. Kilgour, appears to have had a total disinterest in, and, in fact, a hostility toward, the cataloging process, authority control, and the overall notion of the catalog as a coherent whole created in accord with the organizational functions described previously. As a result, OCLC-based libraries are forced to retroactively impose on their catalogs the consistency of entry that was not facilitated and was poorly supported by the OCLC system at the time new catalog records were created, to the extent that it was supported at all.

These libraries are sending their catalogs out for authority-control processing in an effort to establish the consistency of entries that could have been possible had the OCLC system design been concerned with facilitating cataloging rather than card production.

Specifically, OCLC's system design in no way included as its objectives the facilitation of relating editions, translations, and other representations of a work, and relating the works of an author.[2] OCLC, with its multiple forms of an author's name and no references to demonstrate their relatedness, forces the user to do all of the work and research that a sound alphabetic catalog would have made unnecessary.

The user will have to know that *The Melancholy Dane* and *The Prince of Denmark* are other names for the play commonly referred to as *Hamlet*. The user will have to know that Richard Stark is another name under which the popular author Donald Westlake writes.

Of course, the absurd irony is that with OCLC's acquisition of Blackwell/North America's authority-control business, OCLC is now in the position of profiting from the mess it played such a crucial part in creating.

For the uninitiated, libraries whose catalogs have been produced from records derived from OCLC, and such libraries that imposed no systematic relatedness of those records to each other in their local catalogs, gave their catalogs to B/NA to clean up their inconsistencies and variations.

Is the word *cataloging* passé?

Cataloging will never be passé so long as we choose to identify the cataloging enterprise as the construction of bodies of records that help us find not just a library's given publications, but also the various representations of a work or all the works of an author held by the library.

Should the not-so-blessed day occur when nobody gives a damn about the organization of materials in this manner, then *cataloging* indeed will be passé.

Granted, in some respects this has occurred already in the use of the full-text periodical and other databases. The burden, in the cases with which I am familiar, is on the user to figure out how to get the search results sought. Variations in the form of name by which an author is identified may abound. The database suppliers provide no such control. They present the authors' names and article titles simply as they appeared in their published form.[3]

Confusion can abound further with the new online catalogs. The user can do combined searches of the catalog, selected online databases, and even an online encyclopedia depending on the library's turnkey system and subscription services. A well-constructed catalog that provides aids and guidance for the user may not necessarily be carried over to the other resources, but at the minimum it will indicate additional names or words by which to search the database(s).

The future of the word *cataloging* is a different matter. The cataloging courses I taught at Columbia University's former School of Library Service and Pratt Institute were identified as "The Organization of Materials." Using this euphemism and putting cataloging in this broader context is reasonable if one considers that instruction in the applications of the "Dewey Decimal Classification" and the "Sears" and "Library of Congress List of Subject Headings" are also parts of the course syllabus.

I cannot see the word *cataloging* disappear so long as the cataloging enterprise continues. I apologize for the tautological expression of this view, but I would like to think that no other word would be used.

On the other hand, my alma mater, the University of California at Berkeley School of Librarianship, has been replaced by the School of Information Management and Systems. SIMS not only expunged any reference to libraries or librarians from its name, it also eliminated these two words from virtually every course title and description in its, forgive the expression, catalog. Whether the word *cataloging,* as well as the words *library* and *librarian,* will survive such agendas as the current demented efforts of some of the members of the Association of Library and Information Science Educators (ALISE) whose aim is to get rid of the word *library* from the names of the schools that employ them, I do not know.

Having been a Berkeley activist who fought for change, I fear that I have become somewhat of a traditionalist, at least on the issues of the cataloging enterprise and the institution, the library, whose mission it promotes through the organization of its collections. I will oppose the derogation of cataloging, libraries, and librarians into the semantic cesspool[4] to which today's Berkeley SIMS and others assign them.

In conclusion, I would like to quote from my doctoral dissertation, "The Functions of the Catalog and the Main Entry . . ."[5] At the end of the dissertation I wrote the following about the ideology from which the Anglo-American cataloging tradition has been derived:

> These four people, Antonio Panizzi, Charles Coffin Jewett, Charles Ammi Cutter, and Seymour Lubetzky, have created and passed forward a legacy as regards the catalog's functions and their fulfillment. That task is assisted, not eliminated, by the computer. Paraphrasing a Hebrew prayer, I conclude, *Behold the doctrine they have given us, it is a good one.*

NOTES

1. The New York Public Library's authority-control system did not survive the library's own management, but conceptually it lives in and can be found in the Western Library Network (originally the Washington Library Network) system and in many of the turnkey systems being developed or implemented today.

2. Frederick G. Kilgour, the founder of OCLC, asserted that the "mini-cats" created by the results of hash-marked searches obviated the need for the

alphabetic catalog. These mini-cats are the results of searches of the OCLC database based on given combinations of leading alphabetic characters in the words of the title or author's name, and would produce files of records whose sole relatedness is that they matched the criteria of the alphabetic characters selected. The word "mini-cat" as used by Kilgour bears no relation to the "catalog" articulated by Lubetzky and his predecessors, Cutter, Jewett, and Panizzi. When questioned, Kilgour, in this author's presence, has never been able to account for the failure of his mini-cats to demonstrate the relatedness of representations of works and variant author names to each other.

3. Even the accuracy in the databases' presentation of the articles is subject to error because so many of the articles have been converted to machine-readable form by scanners, with little or no human intervention. Anyone who takes the time to read several articles will find typos and weird combinations of letters that do not appear in the articles' original print versions.

4. The first time I heard the phrase *semantic cesspool* was in a comic routine by Lenny Bruce.

5. Maurice J. Freedman, "The Functions of the Catalog and the Main Entry as Found in the Work of Panizzi, Jewett, Cutter and Lubetzky" (Ph.D. diss., Rutgers University, 1983).

10

Cataloging Virtual Libraries

S. MICHAEL MALINCONICO

ibrarians are taking every opportunity to augment their collections with electronic sources. Library users have emphatically endorsed these decisions and have urged them to do even more. Librarians have sought to comply—within the constraints of their budgets. Thus, we are witnessing the rapid development of *digital library collections,* collections that include electronic versions of traditional bibliographic tools, e.g., catalogs, indexes, directories, etc. They also increasingly include the full text of journal and periodical articles, technical reports, and encyclopedias, and less traditional sources such as graphics, pictures, sound recordings, full motion video, etc. Complete issues of journals and the full text of some monographs are also appearing in electronic form in substantial numbers. The universe of materials available in electronic form is steadily expanding. Digital facsimiles of a growing number of rare and noteworthy materials that predate the electronic era are also being created in substantial numbers.

In contrast with traditional resources, libraries often do not own or maintain the electronic sources they make available to their users. Instead, they obtain access rights to them. Users often do not need to go to a library to use many electronic information sources. They can access them from workstations in their homes, offices, or laboratories. Thus, the contents and composition of the *library* one uses become obscure. Instead, the characteristics and identity of the access tools one uses dominate his or her attention. In other words, the relative importance of catalogs and collections is reversed.

Michael Buckland has suggested that collection development librarians partition the universe of conventional library materials into those that by virtue of being acquired are deemed worthy of attention, and all others.[1] This simplistic notion ignores the influence of economics and materials budgets. Nonetheless, Buckland makes the intriguing argument that in an electronic environment a similar division of the universe of information resources may be accomplished not by physical selection but by bibliographic organization. He makes an analogy with Internet gophers in which items that appear in high-level menus are much more readily accessible than those concealed at lower levels of the hierarchy.[2] In such a scheme, cataloging and collection development converge and the traditional distinctions between collection development and cataloging librarians fade.

The idea seems attractive; however, it requires nothing less than a complete reconsideration of our notions of bibliographic control. We would need to develop a system of organization that simultaneously supports information retrieval and hierarchical ordering according to importance. Nonetheless, if this significant hurdle could be overcome, the foregoing model might have considerable appeal. I would like to propose one relatively simple solution that avoids the problem of developing a radically new classification system. But first, let's consider further the nature of virtual collections.

Virtual Data Stores

Workstations connected to a host on the Internet are in principle connected to a global computing resource comprising an aggregate data store of inestimable size. Until recently, this was only an abstraction: an incompletely realized theoretical possibility. A wide variety of workstations and an even greater variety of user interfaces militated against universal access to the myriad resources that are *potentially reachable* via the Internet. The advent of the World Wide Web and Web browsers, however, has brought this ideal closer to realization. Web browsers provide a uniform interface to a vast variety of resources and effectively conceal the technical complexities associated with navigating the Internet in search of them. Browsers create the illusion that the data resources scattered throughout the Internet are a single, immense data store; i.e., they transform the Internet's many discrete databases and data files into a seemingly integrated *virtual* data store.

Virtual Libraries

Because of the scope of the resulting virtual data store resident on the Internet and its relative success in providing answers to certain classes of queries, some have likened it to a *virtual library*. This analogy, however, does not survive close scrutiny. The Internet rather than resembling a library more nearly resembles a bazaar with eclectic collections of old, new, used, duplicated, reassembled, and rebound information sources. The information resources of the Internet fail in several important respects to qualify as a library: they lack the organization, the stability, and the authority of a library collection.

Web Browsers as Filters
and Organizing Media

Web browsers provide a uniform interface to the Internet's numerous resources, and, in addition, they can serve to select and organize those resources. One can assemble and organize a collection of related hyperlinks on a Web page (or on a series of Web pages).[3] Those links can be described and organized in a manner that makes the resources to which they refer far more readily retrieved and used than if they had to be discovered each time de novo. If the links all relate to a common topic, they could be thought to constitute a virtual, special collection on that subject.

I would, therefore, like to propose an organizational and technical structure that will permit us to extract maximum advantage from the emerging networked digital library. While it is not possible to organize the entire contents of the Internet, it is, nonetheless, possible to organize a variety of discipline-specific virtual collections or collections assembled to serve the needs of specific constituencies. In what follows I shall refer to these collections as *focused, virtual collections.*

Focused, virtual collections would consist, in large measure, of links to resources maintained elsewhere—resources that are either free or for which a fee is charged only when they are used, i.e., they generally do not need to be paid for in anticipation of use. This, rather than being a liberating influence, actually calls for greater discipline than is required when assembling physical collections. The value of focused collections is inherent in their small size. When assembling a physical collection, barring fiscal exigencies, we usually prefer to err in favor of *inclusion* rather than exclusion. When assembling a focused, virtual collection, on the other hand, we should prefer to err in favor of *exclusion.* Focused, virtual collections will require maintenance and management. Marginally useful items add to the effort of maintaining the collections without making a commensurate contribution to their usefulness; consequently, they should be avoided.

Development of Focused, Virtual Collections

Teams of subject experts, constituent groups, and catalogers would work together to develop focused, virtual collections. The relative involvement of each may vary. In some instances, subject experts would assemble the collections with consulting advice from catalogers who would also describe and organize the links. In other instances, catalogers—acting in their expanded capacity as developers of collections of information resources—might assume principal responsibility for developing the collections and organizing them with advice from subject experts or representatives of constituent groups.

Catalog librarians who help to assemble focused collections would continue to be responsible for them. They will use their knowledge of Internet resources and search engines to help subject experts discover new or better sources to add to existing collections or to reconstitute links to sources whose addresses have changed. They may also offer guidance on the reliability of resources maintained at particular sites and advice on the cost-effectiveness of those sites that charge fees. They will, in effect, become managers of the virtual collections they help to assemble. This will require intense collaboration with many other individuals. The general availability of electronic mail and other GroupWare tools should make such collaboration practical and efficient.

Librarians as Knowledge Managers

Academic Libraries

Academic librarians already perform some of the foregoing functions. Carla Stoffle, Dean of the University of Arizona libraries, for example, reports on a partnership to redesign instruction at the University of Arizona that includes the library, the computing center, the university faculty, and others. She cites as an outcome the example of a social sciences librarian who worked with a member of the faculty to identify appropriate materials for a Web page to support his anthropology course.[4] They scanned and organized materials for Internet access, including the course syllabus, reading list, full-text articles, and supplemental materials. They also incorporated slides used in class, course notes, audio materials, and links to international resources as well as local support services into the Web page.

This librarian was responsible for assembling not just neutral information resources, but a coherent collection that embodies the *knowledge* that constitutes the anthropology course it supports. A difference between information and knowledge is that knowledge includes context that permits one to make sense of information and permits it to be applied in novel circumstances. Thus, the focused, virtual collections I have described, if properly assembled and organized, would constitute knowledge, rather than information, resources, and by extension the librarians who maintain them would be *knowledge managers.*

Special Libraries

Noteworthy opportunities exist for the exercise of knowledge management in libraries of all types. The most obvious applications will be found in special, or corporate, libraries. Many managers and directors of businesses are gaining a new appreciation for information and knowledge as assets. For example, a former president and CEO of Texas Instruments is quoted as lamenting, "If we only knew what we know."[5] He was expressing regret that knowledge existed in his organization that its employees didn't know about—and therefore weren't using. Often the people who work for organizations don't know what knowledge the organization has or how to find and use it. It is not only necessary to know where an organization's knowledge is but also to realize that it is constantly changing, making it even harder to find.[6] This matter is of sufficient importance that it has gained the interest of many business enterprises. *Fortune* magazine estimates that about 100 of the 500 largest and most successful companies in the United States already employ people who in role, if not always in title, are knowledge officers.[7]

A great deal has been written recently in the management literature—and to a lesser extent in the library literature, too—about chief knowledge officers and their responsibilities. Many business writers seem to agree that the most important responsibility chief knowledge officers have is to create an organizational culture that fosters sharing and reuse of knowledge. This clearly requires high-level management authority. Some librarians and information specialists may advance to such positions. In general, particularly in large organizations, however, we should expect that chief knowledge officers would be selected from among the senior executive ranks. However chosen, chief knowledge officers will need to create organizational and technical structures that facilitate sharing of knowledge. For this they will need to employ various specialists, including information specialists. Librarians, particularly librarians with cataloging expertise, will be leading candidates for these positions.

Recently, the editor of a trade magazine for corporate training officers wrote:

> One of the big surprises turned up by [a study done by the American Productivity and Quality Center] is the extensive range of duties that are required to make knowledge management viable.
>
> Another surprise—or perhaps not—is that one of the more important of these emerging knowledge-support roles, it appears, will fall to . . . and if you are anticipating that I'm going to say the corporate training department here, you're in for a disappointment. No, I'm afraid *the hot ticket in the knowledge management game these days is held by those with a degree in library science.*[8] [Emphasis supplied.]

Librarians, and catalogers in particular, by virtue of their training and experience are uniquely qualified to assume many of the responsibilities of knowledge management, including:

- discovering and retrieving information;
- capturing knowledge, i.e., creating machine-readable documents and moving them onto computer systems;
- adding value to knowledge through editing, packaging, and pruning;

- developing information technology infrastructures and applications for the distribution of knowledge; and
- educating others on the creation, sharing, and use of knowledge.[9]

Intranets as Knowledge Management Tools

Many commercial organizations have established (or will soon establish) *Intranets* to facilitate access to corporate and external information, and communication among their members. Intranets permit members of an organization to access all of its information systems for which Web interfaces have been created from any workstation running a Web browser. These resources are represented and organized as a series of hyperlinks on Web pages.

Some corporate libraries, e.g., those of Arthur Andersen Consulting, BP/Nutrition, General Electric, Hewlett-Packard, McKinsey and Co., Sun Microsystems, and Lotus Development Corporation, have already developed innovative electronic information infrastructures. These systems include a variety of *information* sources, e.g., online catalogs of the traditional print materials they hold and access to internal and external bibliographic databases, such as Dialog, Lexis/Nexis, ABI/Inform, Compendex, etc. But they also include a variety of less traditional knowledge sources, such as:

- directories of information for contacting experts on various matters —a *Yellow Pages of who knows how to do what;*[10]
- directories of discussion groups—some of which may have been set up by the library to deal with specific projects or problems;
- confidential marketing, and competitive intelligence, reports— which the library may have indexed and made more accessible;[11]
- previously prepared documents, e.g., sales presentations, bid responses, and consulting reports—parts of which can be reused in new contexts;[12]
- internally and externally prepared reports of best practices; etc.

The widespread use of computers by commercial enterprises means that they are creating growing stores of electronic information generated by their operational and office support systems. Intranets provide a flexible, cost-efficient means to disseminate this information throughout an organization. They also provide a convenient, common interface that allows simple, integrated access to an organization's stores of information.

Much of this information is an important part of an *organization's memory*. It is not the only part, however, or even the most important part of that memory. Many companies are also concerned with preserving their organizational memory, or organizational knowledge. Thus, they are recording in databases information such as ". . . who did what request for whom, what the nature of the request was, the methodologies used, the costs, and any other ancillary comments for future researchers to learn from."[13] Such databases plus existing stores of operational data constitute a knowledge asset of enormous worth that warrants attentive management.

Intranets permit organizations to make increased use in their normal operations of these often-untapped information resources. But, for these information resources to be useful, they must be organized and indexed; in short, they must be cataloged. No one is better able to do this than the corporate library staff.

Conclusion

Information has never been so readily available or so highly regarded. Electronic information exists that is increasingly able to satisfy many of the information needs people have. Yet, as is readily apparent to anyone who has searched the Internet for information, the Internet is not a library. As with traditional libraries, it will be the professional and intellectual efforts of catalog librarians that impose order on the chaos of the Internet and transform it into a virtual library—or more correctly, virtual collections.

The catalogers who will assemble and organize the focused, virtual collections we have described will need a different set of skills and abilities than their predecessors whose task it was to organize the materials of traditional libraries. They will frequently be dealing with unique material for which no copy cataloging exists. They will need to devise and create unique organizational structures to satisfy specific, local requirements instead of relying on ready-made structures. They will need to create *catalogs, not cataloging records*. They will need to devise rules to govern and guide their work. They will not be able to fall back on simple, catalog-by-example rules.

Ironically, for the past twenty years we have employed a set of cataloging rules that were supposed to be in harmony with electronic technologies. Yet as the technology has matured, we find that the premises underlying those rules may have been faulty. In the pursuit of some chimera of efficiency, the rules have quite simply legislated away difficult intellectual challenges, e.g., the name we give to a work, or the *main entry.* A whole generation of catalogers has been educated and trained to apply rules and to make local situations conform to prevailing norms and standards. Yet we now find that we need individuals who can comprehend principles and who can make rules conform to unique, local conditions.

We do not need clerks who devise cataloging rules. We need a towering intellect that can illuminate cataloging principles that others can apply to solve the numerous, unique information-organization problems a rapidly expanding information universe presents. We have been blessed to have had such a giant in the century that is now drawing to a close. Had we another who could shine the same brilliant light that led us with assurance from the mire of the 1949 rules to the elegance of the 1967 cataloging code, our way to the digital, virtual library would be much more clearly discernable and certain. Maybe a century is not sufficient time to breed more than one such person, for we have in 100 years not known Seymour Lubetzky's equal.

NOTES

1. Michael Buckland, "What Will Collection Developers Do?" *Information Technology and Libraries* 14 (Sept. 1995): 155.

2. Ibid., p. 158.

3. The scheme proposed here resembles the organization of a Yahoo search engine. The idea of using Web browser bookmarks to organize Internet resources was first suggested to me by Steven MacCall. See Steven MacCall, "A Metastrategy for World-Wide Web Information Retrieval in Clinical Medicine," *Medical Reference Quarterly* 16 (Winter 1997): 69–74.

4. Carla J. Stoffle, "The Emergence of Education and Knowledge Management as Major Functions of the Digital Library. Available at: <http://www.ukoln.ac.uk/services/papers/follett/stoffle/paper.html> (accessed 25 May 1999).

5. Carla O'Dell and C. Jackson Grayson, *If We Only Knew What We Know: Identification and Transfer of Internal Best Practices* (Houston, Tex.:

American Productivity & Quality Center, 1997), p. 4. Also available at: <http://www.apqc.org/download/kmpaper.pdf>, accessed May 25, 1999.

6. C. Jackson Grayson, "Taking Inventory of Your Knowledge Management Skills," *Continuous Journey* (American Productivity & Quality Center), Winter 1996. Also available at: <http://www.apqc.org/topics/articles/km01. htm>, accessed May 25, 1999.

7. Thomas A. Stewart, "Is This Job Really Necessary? *Fortune* (12 January 1997): 154.

8. David Stamps, "Managing Corporate Smarts," *Training* 34, no. 8 (August 1997): 40–46.

9. Ibid.

10. Grayson, "Taking Inventory."

11. Kristen Liberman and Jane L. Rich, "Lotus Notes Databases: The Foundations of a Virtual Library," *Online* 16 (June 1993): 39.

12. Ibid., p. 44.

13. Ibid., p. 46.

11

World Wide Web Opportunities in Subject Cataloging and Access

MARCIA J. BATES

We are all aware of the explosive changes in the cataloging world—indeed, the entire world!—because of the extraordinary development of the Internet and various forms of computer and multimedia technology. A great deal of energy has gone into the development of what is known as the Dublin Core[1] and other frameworks for the description of digital information. There is extensive discussion of the character and type of metadata to be appended to electronic documents.

The Dublin Core is probably the best-known proposed set of simplified data elements to be attached to digital records. The Online Computer Library Center (OCLC) has played a major role in its development, and the Core is likely to dominate simplified efforts to describe digital records. The Core's fifteen fields, however, include just one field for the subject matter of the record. (The "title" and "description," or abstract, fields also have subject content though they contain no systematic subject description per se.) So that is it—just one field for "subject."

As if subject were a unitary concept, and all subjects come from the same universe or system of thought! Now I am not arguing for another field in the Core—I know the number of fields must be limited in a deliberately simplified scheme. But I am suggesting that we look closer at the really dramatic new ways we can access materials by subject in the digital environment. If we look harder at such subject access, other modes of access may seem desirable and should be included at this beginning stage of information design for digital records. Those modes may have an impact on the Dublin Core, as well as on other forms of digital information description.

Many of the websites currently available on the World Wide Web are conceptually organized in subtly but significantly different ways from the paper documentary forms of textual information we are accustomed to. The text of a book or article is fundamentally linear, is organized in a line—as in the Latin *filum,* or thread. There is a beginning, a middle, and an end to the thread. We take advantage of that structure by using the contents list or introduction to identify the key concepts for indexing or cataloging purposes.

The reader can, of course, violate the sequentiality of the thread of narrative in a text by dipping into the middle of the text in a codex book or in an article. We do that more, I think, than we realize. I suspect that it is, indeed, because of the desirability of being able to jump in anywhere that, time and again, the codex format has won out over the scroll, whether in vellum, paper, microform, or computer files. Nonetheless, the structure of the book or article is still very linear; for serious reading we normally read straight through front to back, and the *filum,* or thread, metaphor is the most appropriate to current paper document forms.

Much has been made of the hypertextual character of the World Wide Web—how one can jump from one part of a document to another, or from one document to another on the Web. I think less attention has been paid, however, to the changes in the character of the Web document itself, given that one can make these wonderful hypertextual jumps.

When I first looked at the Web, and followed up hypertextual links to other sites, I reminded myself that one can also make jumps within the typical book, so long as it has a back-of-the-book index. For the hypertext links within a site, movement between links is analogous to movement back and forth between a book index and the text of the book. Hypertext is usually faster and easier than hunting terms in indexes and following up the book references in the main text of the book—and that greater ease is very significant to our likelihood of using the hyperlinks—but the logical structure is largely the same.

When, with the hypertext features of the Web, we can also make instant jumps to other documents within the same network matrix, however, a new kind of information organization is made possible. We are beginning to see the early stages of that new form.

In the organization of the Web, I think the new operative metaphor is the structure of our brains—the billions of neurons each with dozens of connections to other neurons all over the brain. As connections can be made easily and quickly to remote sites with dramatically different— but somehow related—content, it is no longer necessary to pound a collection of thoughts, ideas, facts, stories, or illustrations into the linear, rational, organized sequence we are accustomed to in the paper world.

Instead, it is possible to have smaller chunks of information in any one site, connected by hyperlinks to a wide range of other sites, each with related but different information. Such linear order as there is, is created by the reader, who composes a meaningful experience out of the particular sequence of jumps taken through the websites.

This different documentary structure will, sooner or later, lead to diverse types of information units or structures for websites. We are only just beginning to be able to see what those units might be. A website may be dedicated to a famous author, for example. A photo and a very brief biography may be presented, then links are provided to other websites devoted to the discussion of individual works by the author, to the town the writer was born in, to a Nobel Prize site where the text of the Nobel Prize for Literature that was awarded to the author may be found, etc.

Earlier, all these disparate elements might have been drawn together in a single book or article narrative by a scholar or reporter. Now, however, for good or ill, the information user draws together these fragments himself or herself by moving around the Web with the help of the hyperlinks provided by the creator of a website. Once having jumped to another site, the reader can then continue jumping to any other site for which links are provided.

The Web really is creating the kind of information system envisioned by Vannevar Bush in his 1940's Memex system,[2] where the owner of the system could create cross-references anywhere desired between the pieces of information in the system. Bush's vision was for a system that allowed the user/creator of the system to mimic the not-always-logical links that we make in our own minds.

So at least part of the developing model of information on the Web is a structure of neuronlike nodes, or chunks of information, joined by an array of dendrites, or links, to other small nodes or packets of information in the system.

How, then, do we provide subject access to such a structure? We are all familiar with the very real limits of natural or seminatural language searching made available through search engines. It is clear that sooner or later better forms of subject description and access must be found for websites. I do not have a magical solution for this problem, but I do argue that we must recognize the distinct character of websites before we can do the best job at developing good theory and method. The Yahoo approach—a mishmash of sometimes hierarchical, often cross-classified, and occasionally faceted indexing—leaves a lot to be desired.[3]

First, we need to learn more about the various common types of website. There are personal websites and corporate websites for all kinds of organizations. There are websites devoted to cultural phenomena, from famous singers to movies to individual science fiction television programs. There are sites devoted to diseases and their cure, to every hobby and sexual predilection imaginable, sites devoted to famous battles, to genealogy, to animal species, and on and on.

Though eventually every subject matter covered in paper resources will also appear on some websites, I would argue that we may nonetheless find a different distribution overall of subject matter in those sites—more fragmented, small topics—than is typical for the world of books and conventional articles.

Having looked at the subject matter of websites, we would then need to look at the range of types of links. Some research has been conducted on this already, finding links similar to those found in back-of-the-book indexes. I think there is more to be done. Do these links follow the same lines as general mental associations? Is there more freedom and variability in these links, compared to more carefully controlled book index design?

We really do not know nearly enough at this point about the categories of Web link relationships. Chances are that we can find virtually every type of relationship that has already appeared in various forms of subject description. Some would be like subject subdivisions—an author's name followed by subdivisions for biographical information and bibliography would be equivalent to some of the links I described previously for a famous author.

On the other hand, others would have relationships that would not be acceptable as subdivisions, because they are too disparate; they do not fit within our conventional understanding of main topic and subdivisions. In the previous example, the link to the Nobel Prize site would not normally be a subject subdivision.

Another example is a website for a famous Civil War battle that may have links for famous generals of the battle, for the town where it took place, links to casualty figures, and the medical consequences of the war, and so on. On the Web, one can jump to other sites in a mode more closely resembling the web of connections we make in our own day-to-day thinking.

A website for a disease may have links that resemble facets in Ranganathan's sense—diagnosis, cause of disease, and treatment. (Compare Ranganathan's "Medicine" section of his *Colon Classification*. His facets are Organ, Problem (disease), Cause of disease, Handling.[4]) In short, a close examination of Web links is likely to reveal a wide variety of types of links, expressing in turn a variety of implicit modes of classification or categorization.

But how can these ever-so-voluminous links be formalized into a useful way of thinking about how people really think and try to find information, and therefore how subject access can better meet their needs in this new environment? Based on the previous analyses, we might discover that there is a popular set of what might be called *canonical types* of topics for websites. The example given of a famous author might be one such type. More generally, nodes dedicated to a person, dedicated to a work, to a disease or condition, to popular animals, to a city, country, etc., might all be common types.

Each common type of node might in turn have a canonical set of likely links. Link types may resemble facets, too. Or there may be an entirely new way of conceptualizing the nodes and their links—one that truly reflects the neuron/dendrite structure of the World Wide Web.

For example, one way this might work out is: it might be desirable to list the subject or topic of the node itself, then list the link *types,* not necessarily the links themselves, for indexing. The subject metadata for a site on Toni Morrison could show up under the site URL (universal resource locator) in a search engine listing as follows (the hash marks signal that what follows is a link type):

Tony Morrison, brief biography

> #Birthplace #Bibliography #Awards

Another site, on a disease, might appear as follows:

Crohn's Disease, description

> #Support groups #Recommended physicians
>
> #How to recognize #Treatments

A set of link types applied to a given site may be drawn from a larger set, up to, perhaps, thirty types, that are common and appropriate for a site of that type. Thus, the searcher can see how dense the site is with respect to general size (stated in the retrieved record in a Web search) and with respect to links. The searcher can also find desired information indirectly through related sites that lead to a desired site, which is signaled in the link type given in an initial site.

A searcher, for instance, may be trying to find Toni Morrison's birthplace. Indeed, naive online catalog users have been known to enter queries like this: "Toni Morrison birthplace." Needless to say, they receive nothing in conventional catalogs. In a Web search, however, if the searcher enters Morrison's name, the presence of "birthplace" as one of the link types will immediately cue the searcher which of the many retrieved sites should be selected for viewing—*and* will tell the searcher what term to use in a further search. (This mode of searching indirectly, rather than directly, for desired information is known as "scaffolding."[5])

This is just one of the ways that might be found to design indexing for the World Wide Web. Much more needs to be analyzed and experimented with to provide really good indexing for the Web. I think that in the end, the best indexing for the Web will draw on some existing concepts of subject description, but will assemble those concepts in strikingly novel forms of information subject description, forms more reflective of the native associational character of human thought.

NOTES

1. Dublin Core Metadata Initiative, at <http://purl.oclc.org/dc/about/element_set.htm>, accessed April 16, 1999.

2. Vannevar Bush, "As We May Think," *Atlantic Monthly* 176 (July 1945): 101–8.

3. Yahoo!, at <http://www.yahoo.com>, accessed March 26, 1999.

4. S. R. Ranganathan, *Colon Classification,* 6th ed. rev. (London: Asia Publishing House, 1960), pt. 1, p. 88.

5. Marcia J. Bates, "Information Seeking Tactics," *Journal of the American Society for Information Science* 30 (July 1979): 205–14.

12

Cataloging at Crossroads: Preservation and Accommodation

JOHN D. BYRUM, JR.

We at the Library of Congress (LC) view the *Anglo-American Cataloguing Rules,* second edition (AACR2), as one of the greatest monuments to have been crafted in the history of cataloging.[1] Not only did this code bring into general conformance the cataloging practices of North America, the United Kingdom, Australia, and indeed the English-speaking world, but AACR2 has been widely embraced elsewhere—for example, in several European countries and extensively in Latin America. And, significantly, beginning with the mid-1990s, cataloging committees and individual libraries in Germany and Russia, in the Baltic States, in Eastern European countries (including Hungary, Czechoslovakia, and Poland), and in South Africa are expressing strong interest in adopting, adapting, or aligning with AACR2.

Our shared cataloging programs, now brought together under the organization of the Program for Cooperative Cataloging (PCC)—within which more than 250 institutions here and in ten countries abroad contribute name and subject authorities in addition to bibliographic records for monographs and serials—are a further triumph that would not have been possible without widespread agreement on cataloging rules.[2] In the course of preparing for the British Library (BL)'s participation in this program, the LC and BL formally signed a Cataloging Policy Convergence Agreement (CPCA) to achieve at long last an essentially common treatment of rules covering forms of names.[3] Following upon this success, they are continuing their efforts to reconcile differences of rule application and interpretation in other areas as well. The PCC hopes that as a next step the National Library of Canada will subscribe to the CPCA. With the further expansion of the program and thereby the influence of AACR2, similar agreements with other national bibliographic agencies may be realistically anticipated for the twenty-first century.

Many factors explain the ever-increasing popularity of our cataloging approach—in particular, the incredible successes of the bibliographic utilities in encouraging their worldwide constituencies to follow such well-established standards as AACR2. But the code itself must receive the greatest credit for its own success. If the rules did not embody effective principles for the bibliographic control of and access to the innumerable publications now represented in the huge databases of these utilities, long ago we as a profession would have moved on to another approach to achieve bibliographic control. Certainly, Seymour Lubetzky merits the appreciation not only of the thousands of catalogers who apply AACR2, but even more so of the millions of end users who have benefited in retrieving records form catalogs organized according to the principles he imparted.

As a result of 1997's International Conference on the Principles and Future of AACR, however, we are once again embarked on a major review of our cataloging practices.[4] We expect that this exercise will reconfirm much of what is now in the rules by way of basic practices, certainly continuing commitment to the Paris Principles and to the International Standard Bibliographic Descriptions (ISBDs). If so, this would mean that many familiar provisions covering form of headings and description would be in service well into the next century. At the same time, however, we need to acknowledge the possibility if not the likelihood of some changes resulting from this reexamination. This is true because AACR2, although sound overall, is not perfect in all its details, from scarcely anyone's point of view, whether that of practitioner or theorist. It is also true because in many regards the world in which AACR2 first appeared is different in some significant ways from today's bibliographic environment.

During the past quarter century, we have witnessed the metamorphosis of the catalog from a manual and card-based mechanism to one that is now thoroughly computerized. Online public access catalogs have become widespread, while integrated library systems are rapidly becoming the basis for library operations overall. We are connecting the World Wide Web with our online catalogs. Twenty-five years ago, most technical services librarians were focused on print materials—monographs, serials, maps, scores—with varying attention paid to microforms and even some to audiovisual materials. Today, the mix of media represented in most catalogs is much greater than it was when AACR2 was adopted with strong representation of nonbook materials in most cases.

During this period the "machine-readable data file" has also emerged, which soon developed into the "computer file," and now assumes various forms of what is currently covered by the term "electronic resource." Many of these electronic resources have presented unfamiliar features that often do not seem to fit easily into our existing bibliographic framework. This is especially true of remote digital material, where traditional notions of selection, acquisition, cataloging, and preservation simply do not accommodate such "publications."

Indeed, the issue of "content versus carrier" has become a matter of major concern in relation to all electronic publications,[5] while bibliographic problems pertaining to multiple versions of publications in general are much more acute in the 1990s than they were in the 1970s. These developments have promoted a call for reexamination of one of AACR2's cardinal principles, that expressed in Rule 0.24, which stipulates the derivation of bibliographic descriptions from the physical items in hand. Indeed, following the Toronto Conference, the Joint Steering Committee did, in fact, authorize such a reconsideration of this principle.

On this topic, however, there would appear to be no clear-cut preference. When the question is debated by catalogers on the electronic discussion lists, one intuits a strong sentiment in favor of separate records for manifestations of a work, but at the same time, it is clear that many feel the need for a more consolidated approach. One possibility often mentioned is creation of "work records," which would be linked to bibliographic descriptions for different manifestations. Meanwhile, the ALA Committee on Cataloging: Description and Access is preparing a redraft of 0.24, while the Joint Steering Committee is pursuing use of a "data-modeling technique" that may also shed light on this topic.[6]

Technology is impacting on the cataloging rules in another major area as well: seriality. Probably, the paper that produced the greatest agreement at the Toronto Conference was the one authored by Jean

Hirons and Crystal Graham.[7] This presentation thoroughly explored the inadequacy of current approaches to what they call "ongoing publications," whether in print or in electronic format. As a result, Hirons and Graham have been charged to recommend specific changes to AACR2 that conceptually and practically would produce a more effective approach to the bibliographic control for "onging publications," including traditional serials of all kinds, loose-leaf services, and such electronic material as online databases.

A major challenge will be formulation of cataloging policies and rules for works in progress that do not fit the current definition of a serial because they lack successively issued parts. Whether to redefine the term "serial" to incorporate these integrating entities or to take a broader approach to the problems of ongoing works is one major topic now under discussion. Once that question is decided, subsidiary issues will need to be addressed. These range from application of latest and successive entry conventions for title changes, and use of uniform titles, to modification of rules for what constitutes a title change.

While work to sort out the "content versus carrier" and seriality issues progresses, what might be considered by way of more modest and nearer-term efforts to improve AACR2?

Here are some recommendations that have been developed in consultation with descriptive cataloging policy specialists at the Library of Congress *(but are of a personal, not official nature!):*

With regard to Part II, Choice and form of entry, we recommend:

- Review of alternative rules and options, to determine whether some might be dropped. In a cooperative cataloging environment, it is our experience that options and alternatives that do not support collocation of entries are not cost-effective from the viewpoint of the developing global database. This recommendation also has implications for the current AACR2 tendency to allow catalogers to favor "home country"—for example, in selecting uniform titles (25.3C).

- For the same reasons, rules that provide qualifiers for headings and those for resolving conflicting headings should be revisited. These, too, are problematic in the context of a shared database. Perhaps alternatives to existing provisions could be developed that would encourage more uniform results when applied.

- Consideration, in particular, of requiring the application of uniform titles as an AACR2 policy. In today's online catalogs, there is

superior benefit from these collocating devices, much more benefit than was the case with card catalogs. At the Toronto Conference, questions regarding bibliographic relationships loomed
large on the agenda, and this is an area where the data modeling
that the Joint Steering Committee is pursuing should produce improved catalog functionality.

- Reassessment of special rules—especially in Chapter 24, "Headings for Corporate Bodies"—to eliminate any where experience
has shown general rules are adequate to cover the situations with
which they deal.

- Revisiting the rules for "Works of Mixed Responsibility" (21.8–
21.27) to see if adjustments need to be made to address various
concerns raised by catalogers of motion pictures and video-
recordings and other specialists dealing with media prominent in
this area.

- Continuing the so-called case-law rules but in a scaled-down version. This recommendation reflects our belief that they are useful
to generalist catalogers who occasionally have to process reli-
gious, legal, or musical works. On the other hand, detailed rules
to deal with the more complicated aspects, appropriate to specialist catalogers, should be removed to authorized manuals prepared
by designated librarian groups, as authorized by the Joint Steering
Committee.

- Eliminating card catalog–based terminology and reformulating as
necessary the provisions to which they are applied. The instruction "make a title-added entry for . . ." that frequently appears in
Part II is one of several examples to which this recommendation
pertains.

In the descriptive area, we suggest:

- Reconsideration of the placement of the general material designation (GMD). Is it still necessary to intrude this data element in the
midst of the transcription for the title and statement of responsibility as an "early alert"? Or is that practice a holdover from an
era when nonbook materials were sparsely represented in the card
catalog? If it does prove necessary to retain the GMDs, at least we
should attempt to reconcile the two lists of such designations that
now coexist in AACR2. Recent experience in formulating the *International Standard Bibliographic Description for Electronic*

Resources serves as an example of how it proved possible to develop a single set of suitable terms for designations that are acceptable to a wide variety of users both here and abroad.[8]

- Similarly, examination of the relationship between the GMDs and the specific material designations (SMDs) to determine whether both are still needed or whether the SMDs might be sufficient in themselves to characterize the nature of the item being described.

- Reduction of abbreviations allowed in the bibliographic description. Even within an English-speaking country, end users are so diverse today that abbreviations are often misunderstood, and the need to compact descriptions to the extent possible is not the major consideration in an online catalog that it was in the card catalog.

- Reevaluate specifications for the three levels of description stipulated in Rule 1.0D. With the recent publication of the recommendations of the International Federation of Library Associations and Institutions (IFLA) Working Group on *Functional Requirements for Bibliographic Records,* the components for a base-level national record have now emerged.[9] As a result of the ongoing work of the PCC Standards Committee, the specifications for core-level records for various formats are also being issued.[10] Therefore, perhaps in place of the existing three levels in AACR2, these two possibilities should be introduced, allowing any cataloging agency to include additional data at any level given when it desires to do so.

- Increased reliance on cataloger's judgment in matters where uniformity is not essential by seeking opportunities to make the rules for description more suggestive and less directive; for example, in the notes area.

Beyond such possibilities for seeking modest improvements to AACR2 that might prove relatively easy to formulate and implement, two procedural issues will need attention in the near term. First, with technology fostering growth of international interest in the code is increased representation for practices known to new and prospective constituents but which are now outside existing rules. Also, these new or potential stakeholders will surely desire a greater role in the revision process than is now available to them. Second, speaking of the revision process, clearly it would benefit from simplification and from greater efforts to speed up reaching consensus on the parts of the authors, so that AACR2 can become more adaptable in coping with changing conditions than has been the case for some time. More effective review and maintenance mechanisms will help to assure the continued relevance and viability of AACR2 and thus to preserve into the next millennium what Michael Gorman and Pat Oddy have called the "Lubetzkyan ideas that are at the core of the rules."[11]

NOTES

1. Michael Gorman and Paul W. Winkler, eds., *Anglo-American Cataloguing Rules,* 2nd ed., 1998 revision (Ottawa: Canadian Library Association; Chicago: American Library Association, 1998). "Prepared under the direction of the Joint Steering Committee for Revision of AACR."

2. For a description of the Program for Cooperative Cataloging, its governance, accomplishments, and component programs (NACO, SACO, CONSER, BIBCO), visit its website at <http://lcweb.loc.gov/catdir/pcc>, accessed May 25, 1999.

3. For more details, visit <http://lcweb.loc.gov/catdir/pcc/converge.html>, accessed May 25, 1999.

4. For the origins and outcomes of the Conference, visit the Joint Steering Committee's website at <http://www.nlc-bnc.ca/jsc/index.htm>, accessed May 25, 1999. The papers presented are published in Jean Weihs, ed., *The Principles and Future of AACR: Proceedings of the International Conference on the Principles and Future Development of AACR, Toronto, Ontario, Canada, October 23–25, 1997* (Ottawa: Canadian Library Association; London: Library Association Publishing; Chicago: American Library Association, 1998).

5. For an overview of the issue, see Lynne C. Howarth, "Content versus Carrier," in *Principles and Future of AACR,* 148–56.

6. This topic was discussed in detail at the Toronto Conference by Tom Delsey in his paper "Modeling the Logic of AACR," in *Principles and Future of AACR,* 1–16.

7. Jean Hirons and Crystal Graham, "Issues Related to Seriality," in *Principles and Future of AACR,* 180–212.

8. *ISBD(ER): International Standard Bibliographic Description for Electronic Resources,* UBCIM Publications, New Series, vol. 17 (Munich: K. G. Saur, 1997).

9. *Functional Requirements for Bibliographic Records: Final Report,* UBCIM Publications, New Series, vol. 19 (Munich: K. G. Saur, 1998), available on the Internet at <http://www.ifla.org/ifla/VII/s13/frbr/frbr.pdf>, accessed May 25, 1999.

10. See the Program for Cooperative Cataloging's website at Note 2.

11. Michael Gorman and Pat Oddy, "The Anglo-American Cataloguing Rules, Second Edition: Their History and Principles," in *Principles and Future of AACR,* 159.

13

Guidelines for a Future Anglo-American Cataloging Code

MARGARET F. MAXWELL

Because of Seymour Lubetzky and his once "radical" ideas, I became a cataloging teacher, so thoroughly grounded in Lubetzky's principles and philosophy that in the period between AACR (1967) and AACR2 (1978) I formulated a written series of explanations of problems and principles governing AACR for my students. This evolved into the first edition of my *Handbook for AACR2*,[1] designed to explain the rules not only for students of cataloging but for inexperienced catalogers in the field. I'm pleased to say that the *Handbook* proved useful enough to go through several revised editions, the latest by my son, Robert L. Maxwell.[2]

Yet despite the fact that I followed Seymour Lubetzky for a number of years, I did not actually meet him until 1967. He received his library degree from the University of California at Berkeley in 1934; I got mine in 1950. I went from Berkeley to the Library of Congress (LC) as an intern that same year. Lubetzky, who had been at LC seven years before I arrived, was about to be appointed Consultant on Bibliographic and Cataloging Policy with a charge to "make a study of the rules for descriptive cataloging . . . and to formulate the objectives and principles upon which a revision of the [1949 A.L.A.] rules should be based."[3]

As the most junior of junior LC catalogers in the five years that followed my internship, I was aware of Lubetzky and his work, but though
I probably passed him more than once in the halls of the Library of
Congress, it would never have occurred to me to strike up an acquain-
tance with him.

In 1956, I left the Library of Congress for a position as Associate Librarian in charge of Technical Processes and Instructor in English and
Library Science at Upper Iowa University, where I remained for the next
twelve years. Lubetzky, meanwhile, was lured away from the Library of
Congress in 1960 by the dean of the new UCLA Library School, none
other than our good friend Larry Powell, to begin his career as teacher
of cataloging. I'd like to have sat in on his classes. I can hardly believe he
would have taught the then current 1949 ALA Rules without critiquing
them vigorously, combining this with suggestions for a more rational,
unified way of describing and controlling library collections. For when
Lubetzky came to UCLA he had just completed his radically new *Code
of Cataloging Rules: Author and Title Entry: An Unfinished Draft,* presented at the Montreal Institute in June of 1960.[4] A year later, this same
code served as the basis for discussion at the International Conference
on Cataloguing Principles (Paris, 1961), resulting in the *Statement of
Principles* that forms the foundation of our *Anglo-American Cataloguing Rules* today.[5]

Those must have been heady days, both for Seymour Lubetzky and
for his students at the UCLA Library School. But although I began to
teach the 1967 *Anglo-American Cataloging Rules* as soon as they were
published,[6] I did not meet the man responsible in large part for them
until I enrolled in his seminar entitled "Cataloging: Purposes, Problems,
Principles," offered as a special course between July 17 and August 12,
1967, on the University of Illinois campus at Urbana-Champaign.

Seymour Lubetzky's four-week seminar proved to be a defining moment in my professional career. The course began with Panizzi and the
1841 British Museum Rules[7] and continued with American cataloging
rule makers such as Charles Coffin Jewett and Charles Ammi Cutter.
After our daily lecture we were turned loose in the great University of
Illinois library to read from an extensive bibliography of original source
documents, which I devoured joyfully.

Intermixed with his lectures on cataloging history, Lubetzky discussed rules and principles of cataloging, leading us logically through the
theoretical basis for bibliographic control that he himself had arrived at

through years of thought and study, and that finally resulted in the then new 1967 *Anglo-American Cataloging Rules*. What a mind-expanding month this was for me! I finished his seminar with a grasp of cataloging theory and the ability to understand and explain cataloging rules to my students as I never had been able to do before.

Once started, I had to know more. The following year I entered the doctoral program at the University of Michigan. On the completion of my degree in 1971, I joined the faculty of what was then called the Graduate Library School at the University of Arizona to begin a quarter century of research, teaching, and writing.

And now to my topic: guidelines for a future cataloging code, be it a revision of AACR2 or a radically different rethinking of cataloging theory that might properly be called AACR3. And by the way, I do not favor an AACR3. As one who remembers all too well the AACR2 wars of the late 1970s, I agree with Michael Gorman in his preference for "evolutionary . . . [rather than] revolutionary change" in cataloging.[8]

So what should the new AACR include? In the first place, I think those who craft such an instrument should keep the features that impressed me so favorably when I first saw the preliminary AACR2 in the mid-1970s. AACR2 is organized in a beautifully logical fashion, starting in Part I with rules for the description of the item, which regardless of type of media is to be based on formats mandated by International Standard Bibliographic Descriptions (ISBDs). A general chapter is followed by chapters giving rules for specific types of materials, each rule keyed to the rules in the first chapter. This emphasizes the fact that all materials are to be described according to the same principles.

Only after the item has been described does the cataloger consider appropriate access points according to rules given in Part II. Once again, the logical structure of the code is impeccable, moving from choice of access points (Chapter 21) to the form of the resulting names (Chapters 22 and following).

Incidentally, however, I still remember how startled I was in the 1970s when I first read 22.1, the general rule under "Headings for Persons," to find names printed in direct, rather than cataloging, order, e.g., Jimmy Carter rather than Carter, Jimmy. Because I knew that AACR2 was in many respects a radically different code, my first reaction was that traditional surname-forename order had been abolished! Yes, of course, I shortly figured out what was going on. But because I had been momentarily taken aback, I made sure that I included a cautionary explanation of Chapter 22's organization in the *Handbook*. I think perhaps in this instance the editors carried their impeccable logic a little too far—lacking any explanation in the paragraph that begins AACR2 22.1. Well, perhaps that is one reason why the *Handbook* has proved to be useful.

The rest of my suggestions for the most part reiterate some of the ideas put forth by speakers at the International Conference on the Principles and Future Development of AACR held in Toronto, October 23 to 25, 1997, that I particularly agree with. To begin with first things, a new general introduction to AACR needs to be written, clearly setting forth the principles on which the rules are based. At a minimum, because it remains the foundation document for AACR, the "Statement of Principles adopted at the International Conference on Cataloguing Principles, Paris, October 1961," should be summarized in this introduction. (This statement is summarized in the introduction to the *Handbook*.) In addition, because Seymour Lubetzky's ideas form the basis for most of the rules, I would like to see an explicit statement to this effect, perhaps including a summary, if not the entire text, of the objectives and principles which Lubetzky set forth in his *Code of Cataloging Rules*.[9]

Of course, were Lubetzky's principles emphasized, it would logically follow that some of the holdovers from pre-AACR rules that are still imbedded in AACR2 (what Gorman calls "case-law hangovers") should be removed. I am reminded of the Mikado's Lord High Executioner and his "little list" of undesirables. These "pestilential nuisances . . . they'd none of 'em be missed!"

I found it heartening to learn that despite a continued undercurrent of dissatisfaction with the concept of main entry, the Toronto Conference did not recommend a change in current rules. I agree with Martha Yee's eloquent plea for keeping the principle of main entry as presented in an online discussion group on the Toronto Conference papers.[10] Perhaps I would stop short of saying, as she did, that it would be "an act of cultural vandalism to jettison the main entry,"[11] but I think that though some of the traditional reasons for emphasizing main entry may have lesser importance with the increasing dominance of the online catalog, it is still necessary when citing a given work (as required for subject entries and entries for related works).

One of the topics I remember most distinctly from Seymour Lubetzky's 1967 cataloging seminar was his repeated discussion of the concept of a work as distinguished from an edition, translation, or other version of an item. As was emphasized in Martha Yee's Toronto Conference paper, "What Is a Work?",[12] further study is needed to clarify this distinction. To do this, a clear definition of a "work" needs to be formulated. Should the new code move in the direction of cataloging the "work" rather than the individual item? And if so, should the rules mandate the use of uniform titles rather than suggesting they be applied "according to the policy of the cataloguing agency" (AACR2 25.1)? These are all matters which as we move further in the direction of international acceptance of AACR in the English-speaking cataloging world must be carefully considered.

NOTES

1. Margaret F. Maxwell, *Handbook for AACR2: Explaining and Illustrating Anglo-American Cataloguing Rules, Second Edition* (Chicago: American Library Association, 1980).

2. Robert L. Maxwell with Margaret F. Maxwell, *Maxwell's Handbook for AACR2: Explaining and Illustrating the Anglo-American Cataloguing Rules and the 1993 Amendments* (Chicago: American Library Association, 1997).

3. Seymour Lubetzky, *Cataloging Rules and Principles: A Critique of the A.L.A. Rules for Entry and a Proposed Design for Their Revision* (Washington, D.C.: Library of Congress, 1953; reprint, High Wycombe, England: Published for the College of Librarianship, Wales, by University Microfilms, 1970), p. v.

4. Seymour Lubetzky, *Code of Cataloging Rules: Author and Title Entry: An Unfinished Draft for a New Edition of Cataloging Rules, Prepared for the Catalog Code Revision Committee,* with an explanatory commentary by Paul Dunkin (Chicago: American Library Association, 1960).

5. International Conference on Cataloguing Principles, *Statement of Principles Adopted at the International Conference on Cataloguing Principles, Paris, October 1961,* annotated ed. with commentary and examples, ed. Eva Verona (London: British Museum; International Federation of Library Associations (Committee on Cataloguing), 1971).

6. *Anglo-American Cataloging Rules. North American Text* (Chicago: American Library Association, 1967).

7. "Rules for the Compilation of the Catalogue," in British Museum, Dept. of Printed Books, *Catalogue of Printed Books in the British Museum* (London:

Printed by Order of the Trustees, 1841), vol. 1, p. v–ix; reprinted in *Foundations of Cataloging: A Sourcebook,* ed. Michael Carpenter and Elaine Svenonius (Littleton: Colo.: Libraries Unlimited, 1985), p. 3–14.

8. Michael Gorman and Pat Oddy, "The Anglo-American Cataloguing Rules, Second Edition: Their History and Principles," in Jean Weihs, ed., *The Principles and Future of AACR: Proceedings of the International Conference on the Principles and Future Development of AACR, Toronto, Ontario, Canada, October 23–25, 1997* (Ottawa: Canadian Library Association; London: Library Association Publishing; Chicago: American Library Association, 1998), p. 163.

9. Lubetzky, *Code of Cataloging Rules,* p. ix–xv.

10. Contributions to the online discussion may be found at the Joint Steering Committee's website, <http://www.nlc-bnc.ca/jsc/index.htm>, under "Discussion List Archives." See Martha Yee's message dated September 10, 1997, accessed April 9, 1999.

11. Ibid., October 6, 1997, accessed April 9, 1999.

12. Martha M. Yee, "What Is a Work?", in Weihs, *The Principles and Future of AACR,* p. 62–104. See also Chapter 7, "Lubetzky's Work Principle," by Martha M. Yee.

14

Current Activities in Cataloging Code Revision

BARBARA B. TILLETT

I'd like to review the current activities in code revision going on within the Library of Congress, within the Anglo-American community, and internationally. Then I'll review some of the extraordinary insights presented at the Lubetzky Symposium.

Library of Congress Activities for Code Revision

The Library of Congress (LC) has been involved this entire century and before in the process of documenting cataloging rules and revising them. We are currently working on several fronts to review the basic structure of the bibliographic universe with a goal of structuring the cataloging rules to better meet the challenges of the future, following a principle-based approach, as recommended by Seymour Lubetzky. We are reviewing internal rule interpretations, working with international groups that are revising their cataloging rules, and we continue working as active participants in the rule revision process for the *Anglo-American Cataloguing Rules*.

The Library of Congress, serving as the national library for the United States, provides standards for cataloging, rule interpretations, and cataloging tools to libraries throughout the world, creating or using records following the *Anglo-American Cataloguing Rules* and US-MARC formats. These standards and guidelines are also used by our partners in cooperative programs such as Name Authority Cooperative Program (NACO) and now the Program for Cooperative Cataloging (PCC). We recently completed a review of the *Library of Congress Rule Interpretations* (LCRIs) for chapters 0, 1, 2, and 12, eliminating many rule interpretations and updating others.

The LCRIs were originally intended as guidance to LC's own catalogers—nearly 600 people—to provide consistency in our cataloging products. Other cooperative programs have incorporated the use of these rule interpretations into their standards as well, but the LCRIs continue to receive criticism for not allowing much cataloger judgment.

Our efforts at rule revision were slowed down through 1999 as we implemented a new integrated library system (ILS). This is a major undertaking for the library, involving nearly 3,000 staff members. The results will be an integrated system that is Year 2000 compliant, addresses our needs to improve inventory control, provides the opportunity for business process improvements, and provides a platform for moving us into the next century with new technologies.

Joint Steering Committee Update

As a member of the Joint Steering Committee (JSC) for revision of the *Anglo-American Cataloguing Rules,* I represent the Library of Congress and coordinate LC's submission of proposals for changes to the cataloging rules. The rule revision process has been criticized for being too slow. This system, however, allows considered review before changes are made. The JSC held an international conference in Toronto, October 23 to 25, 1997, to review the underlying principles on which the rules are based and to discuss the future of the rules. The outcome of the conference has been published.[1]

The JSC identified the following action items during the conference and reported on the progress:

Data modeling

>Tom Delsey was contracted as a consultant to prepare an analysis of AACR2R in light of the data model presented in the International Federation of Library Associations and Institutions (IFLA) *Functional Requirements for Bibliographic Records.*[2] His report is available at the JSC website.[3]

Principles

>The Conference was supposed to document the underlying principles, but it did not. The JSC will now take on the task of identifying those principles.

Seriality recommendations

>Several recommendations regarding the ongoing nature of publications were examined and proposals made to follow up with recommended changes to the rules to incorporate the concept of seriality.

Rule 0.24 revision proposal

>The "cardinal rule" of cataloging based on the item in hand was found to be too literal and in need of change, given the expanding universe of electronic and digital materials. The American Library Association was charged with proposing new wording for this rule.

AACR website

>A permanent website for information regarding rule revision process and activities was proposed as an extension of the website established for the conference. That site is now in place.[4]

Mission statement for the JSC

>The JSC will spend time at its next meeting developing a mission statement, so that its purpose is clear to everyone.

Survey of the use of AACR2 outside Anglo-American community

>Australia will take on a review of the literature to determine any existing studies of the use of AACR2R outside the Anglo-American community and we will make such information known, if it already exists, and prepare a survey, if none yet exists.

The JSC is also working with the publishers of the *Anglo-American Cataloguing Rules* to produce a print compilation of the second edition, revised with all the amendments to date.[5] Also, the long-awaited electronic version of AACR-e should be available this year.

International Code Review

This is a truly remarkable time for cataloging rules, much like the atmosphere that led to the Paris Principles that Seymour Lubetzky was so instrumental in bringing about. Several countries that have had their own cataloging rules for many years are now reviewing those rules in light of the economics of reducing cataloging costs through sharing cataloging records in machine-readable form. In Germany, the *Regeln für alphabetische Katalogisierung* (RAK) has been compared to AACR2R and great strides have been made to bring RAK more in line with AACR2R. Also, recommendations on changes to AACR2R have come from the RAK rule makers and will be reviewed by the JSC. A similar effort in Russia at the National Library of Russia in St. Petersburg has led to recommendations for rule changes to bring rules closer into harmony. The Library of Congress and the Online Computer Library Center (OCLC) have been involved in several projects with these groups to promote closer alignment of rules.

This spirit of rule review also reached IFLA. Starting several years ago with the IFLA Standing Committee on Cataloging's Study Group on the Functional Requirements for Bibliographic Records, the analysis of essential information in cataloging records has driven several projects. There is a strong recognition of the need to modify the IFLA concept of "Universal Bibliographic Control." That concept involved everyone in the world using the same set of headings as established by national bibliographic agencies. It is now clear that important reasons exist for diversity, such as differences in languages, scripts, and cultural variances that make it important to focus more on the needs of local users than on global consistency. With this in mind, three IFLA working groups are reviewing IFLA guidelines and proposing changes that will ultimately impact cataloging rules. The IFLA UBCIM (Universal Bibliographic Control and International MARC Program) Working Group on Minimal Level Authority Records and the International Standard Authority Data Number has prepared a report on the mandatory data elements needed in shared authority records. The IFLA Standing Committee on Cataloguing's two working groups are looking at updating IFLA guidelines related to corporate headings[6] and authority and reference entries.[7] These working groups should have their work completed next year. A definite air of optimism and positive feelings of cooperation predominate the cataloging world today.

Areas for Future Work

This now brings us to the observations and insights from the Lubetzky Symposium. To briefly summarize those areas targeted for comment:

Main and added entry

- Whether we have main entries in the future or not, we need to keep in mind that access points are a means to fulfill objectives of the catalog.

Cataloging guidelines

- These need to focus on purposes, problems, and principles.
- We must look within the library versus beyond.

What from the past codes should be carried forward for future codes?

- Opposite recommendations were made both to get rid of ISBDs and to continue our commitment to them.
- We need to accommodate new and variant forms of information.
- It was recommended that we embed URLs (universal resource locators) in authority records.
- We need to make changes for seriality.
- We need to reduce alternative rules.
- We need to apply uniform titles.
- We should reassess special rules.
- We must eliminate card-based terminology.
- We should review the general material designations/special material designations.
- We should minimize the use of abbreviations.

- The relative importance of the catalog and the collections reverses in the future with
  - access to global resources and
  - focused, virtual collections.
- Knowledge managers will be needed with degrees in library science.

The Lubetzky legacy has given us principle-based cataloging. It is a rich legacy based on intellectual integrity with continuous challenging of the rules. It is a legacy that recognizes that cataloging is essential to the use of information. Without the bibliographic control that cataloging brings, the ever-increasing mass of information is mere chaos.

NOTES

1. Jean Weihs, ed., *The Principles and Future of AACR: Proceedings of the International Conference on the Principles and Future Development of AACR, Toronto, Ontario, Canada, October 23–25, 1997* (Ottawa: Canadian Library Association; London: Library Association Publishing; Chicago: American Library Association, 1998).

2. *Functional Requirements for Bibliographic Records: Final Report,* UBCIM Publications, New Series, vol. 19 (Munich: K. G. Saur, 1998), available on the Internet at <http://www.ifla.org/ifla/VII/s13/frbr/frbr.pdf>, accessed May 25, 1999.

3. Part I at <http://www.nlc-bnc.ca/jsc/aacrdel.htm>, Part II at <http://www.nlc-bnc.ca/jsc/aacrdel2.htm>, accessed May 25, 1999.

4. At <http://www.nlc-bnc.ca/jsc/index.htm>, accessed May 25, 1999.

5. *Anglo-American Cataloguing Rules,* 2nd ed., 1998 revision (Ottawa: Canadian Library Association; London: Library Association Publishing; Chicago: American Library Association, 1998).

6. International Federation of Library Associations and Institutions, Working Group on Corporate Headings, *Form and Structure of Corporate Headings: Recommendations of the Working Group on Corporate Headings* (London: IFLA International Office for UBC, 1980).

7. International Federation of Library Associations and Institutions, Working Group on an International Authority System, *Guidelines for Authority and Reference Entries* (London: IFLA International Programme for UBC, 1984).

CONTRIBUTORS

Marcia J. Bates is Professor in the UCLA Department of Information Studies. Her research interests include information search strategy, information-seeking behavior, user-centered design of information retrieval systems and interfaces, subject access, and science and technology information services. Recent work includes a project with the Getty Research Institute for the History of Art and the Humanities to determine the multimedia hardware and software support provided by museums, universities, and libraries to scholars. She is also editing the Fiftieth Anniversary issue of the *Journal of the American Society for Information Science.*

John D. Byrum, Jr., Chief of the Regional and Cooperative Cataloging Division at the Library of Congress, was Head Cataloger, Princeton University, until 1977, when he joined the LC staff as Chief, Descriptive Cataloging Division; he also served as Acting Chief, Subject Cataloging Division from 1988 until 1992 when he assumed his current position. He holds the Esther J. Piercy Award, is the 1998 recipient of the Margaret Mann Citation, Secretariat of the Program for Cooperative Cataloging, member of the IFLA Section on Bibliography, and Honorary member of the IFLA Section on Cataloguing. He is also chair of the ISBD Review Committee and of the ISBD project group that recently completed production of the International Standard Bibliographic Description for Electronic Resources. He was chair of the ALA Catalog Code Revision Committee that contributed to production of AACR2 and has held several positions in the Association for Library Collections and Technical Services.

Allyson Carlyle is Assistant Professor at the School of Library and Information Science, University of Washington, Seattle. Her research interests include use and display of cataloging information in online catalogs and conceptual foundations of descriptive cataloging.

Michael Carpenter received his M.L.S. in 1967 from UCLA, where he studied cataloging with Seymour Lubetzky. After a stint as a serials cataloger at the Library of Congress, he began his doctoral studies under Patrick Wilson at UC Berkeley, where he received a Ph.D. in 1979 with a conceptual-historical dissertation on corporate authorship. In 1985 he edited *Foundations of Cataloging: A Sourcebook* with Elaine Svenonius, and then joined the faculty at the School of Library and Information Science, Louisiana State University, in 1987, where he is now an Associate Professor.

Michèle V. Cloonan is Chair and Associate Professor in the UCLA Department of Information Studies. She has published widely in the areas of preservation and book trade history.

Tschera Harkness Connell, Serials Coordinator for the Ohio State University Libraries, was on the faculty of the Kent State University School of Library and Information Science for eight years prior to recently joining the OSU staff. She taught courses in cataloging, collection management, database design theory, and indexing. Her Ph.D. in library and information science is from the University of Illinois at Urbana-Champaign. Her research examines the effects of information organization theory and practice on retrieval.

Maurice J. Freedman has had technical services managerial positions at the Library of Congress, Information Dynamics Corp., Hennepin (Minn.) County Library, and the New York Public Library, and currently is the Director of the Westchester (N.Y.) Library System. He also was an Associate Professor at Columbia University's School of Library Service and at present teaches at Pratt Institute as an adjunct associate professor. Among his honors are his selection to the Library of Congress's Special Recruit Program for Outstanding Library School Graduates, and the LITA Award for Outstanding Achievement in Library and Information Technology. He has been a consultant on information technology and on public libraries on four continents.

Michael Gorman is Dean of Library Services at the Henry Madden Library, California State University, Fresno. He is the first editor of the *Anglo-American Cataloguing Rules,* second edition (1978) and the revision of that work (1988); the author of three editions of *The Concise*

AACR2 (1980, 1989, 1999); editor of *Crossroads* and of *Convergence,* the proceedings of the first two LITA National Conferences; editor of and contributor to both editions of *Technical Services Today and Tomorrow* (1990 and 1998); co-author of *Future Libraries: Dreams, Madness and Reality* (1995); author of *Our Singular Strengths* (1997); and author of more than 150 articles in professional and scholarly publications. Gorman is a fellow of the [British] Library Association, the 1979 recipient of the Margaret Mann Citation, and the 1992 recipient of the Melvil Dewey Award.

Sara Shatford Layne earned an M.F.A. (Stanford, 1972) and worked for nine years as a theatrical costume designer before becoming a librarian (M.L.S., UCLA, 1982). She then worked at the Pierpont Morgan Library in New York, cataloging early children's books, before returning to UCLA in 1984 to pursue her doctoral studies in library and information science and to work first as a cataloger and then (and currently) as head of the Cataloging Division in the UCLA Science and Engineering Library. She completed her Ph.D. in 1997. She is interested in many aspects of cataloging, but particularly in the problems of cataloging image materials.

Gregory H. Leazer is Assistant Professor in the UCLA Department of Information Studies, where he teaches courses related to the organization of information. His research interests include bibliographic control, bibliographic works and relationships, cataloging, and the evaluation of information retrieval systems.

Seymour Lubetzky, the honoree of the symposium and foremost cataloging theorist of the twentieth century, was born April 28, 1898, in Zelwa, Poland (then part of Russia). In 1927, he emigrated to the United States, settling in Los Angeles. He received a B.A. from UCLA in 1931, followed by a master's degree in German and a secondary teaching credential from UC Berkeley in 1932. In 1934 he received the graduate Certificate of Librarianship from UC Berkeley and, shortly thereafter, began a brilliant cataloging career that spanned thirty-five years, making his mark first as a member of the UCLA library staff, then for seventeen years as a bibliographical specialist in the Library of Congress, and finally returning to UCLA in 1960 as a professor in the newly established School of Library Service. Lubetzky came to national prominence for his reasoned and principled criticism of existing cataloging rules. His writings provided the basis for the "Paris Principles," formulated at the 1961 International Conference on Cataloguing Principles in Paris; the results of the Paris Conference ultimately led to the development of the *Anglo-American Cataloguing Rules*. Honors awarded to Lubetzky during his illustrious career include the Margaret Mann Citation (1955), the Beta Phi Mu Award for Good Teaching (1965), a Doctor of Laws degree (UCLA, 1969), and the Melvil Dewey Award (1977).

S. Michael Malinconico, currently the endowed EBSCO chair in library and information studies at the University of Alabama, holds master's degrees in physics and library service from Columbia University. Former Dean of the Pratt Institute School of Computing, Information, and Library Sciences, he was also Associate Director for Technical and Computer Services at the New York Public Library. He has written more than seventy articles on cataloging, library management, and the use of electronic technologies in libraries. His publications appear in numerous professional journals throughout the world. He has coauthored two monographs on library catalogs.

Margaret F. Maxwell, Professor Emerita, School of Information Resources and Library Science, University of Arizona, is the original author of the *Handbook for AACR2* (1980, 1989, 1993), reissued by ALA in 1997 with extensive revisions by her son, Robert L. Maxwell. She is the recipient of the 1991 Margaret Mann Citation for her work in descriptive cataloging and teaching. Her prize-winning publications and research in Arizona history were recently recognized at the joint Arizona/New Mexico Historical Society Conference, where she received the Sharlot Hall Award for her work as historian, writer, and teacher.

Robert L. Maxwell, author of the current edition of *Maxwell's Handbook for AACR2* (1997), is Associate Librarian at the Harold B. Lee Library, Brigham Young University, where he catalogs special collections and ancient languages materials. He has taught cataloging at the University of Arizona Graduate School of Library Science and currently chairs the Bibliographic Standards Committee of the Rare Books and Manuscripts Section of the Association of College and Research Libraries.

Elaine Svenonius has taught and written widely in the areas of cataloging, classification, and indexing, with a particular interest in theory.

Currently, she is working on a book on the intellectual foundation of information organization. She is the 1992 recipient of the Margaret Mann Citation.

Barbara B. Tillett is Director for the Integrated Library System Program and Chief of the Cataloging Policy and Support Office of the Library of Congress. Her Ph.D. in library and information science is from the University of California, Los Angeles.

Martha M. Yee is Cataloging Supervisor at the UCLA Film and Television Archive and coauthor, with Sara Shatford Layne, of *Improving Online Public Access Catalogs,* published by the American Library Association in 1998.

INDEX

DATE DUE
